The Kind of Brave You Wanted to Be

The Kind of Brave
You Wanted to Be

Prose Prayers and Cheerful Chants against the Dark

Brian Doyle

LITURGICAL PRESS
Collegeville, Minnesota

www.litpress.org

1	2	3	4	5	6	7	8	9

Library of Congress Cataloging-in-Publication Data

Names: Doyle, Brian, 1956 November 6– author.
Title: The kind of brave you wanted to be : prose prayers and cheerful chants against the dark / Brian Doyle.
Description: Collegeville, Minnesota : Liturgical Press, 2016.
Identifiers: LCCN 2016009626 (print) | LCCN 2016024494 (ebook) | ISBN 9780814646519 (softcover) | ISBN 9780814646755 (ebook)
Subjects: | BISAC: RELIGION / Christianity / Literature & the Arts. | POETRY / Inspirational & Religious. | POETRY / American / General.
Classification: LCC PS3604.O9547 A6 2016 (print) | LCC PS3604.O9547 (ebook) | DDC 818/.6—dc23
LC record available at https://lccn.loc.gov/2016009626

For my friend Martin Joseph Flanagan of Launceston, Tasmania, with gratitude for years of friendship and laughter and storytelling and storycatching. Deartháir go raibh maith agat, cousin.

Maybe that's the true power of words —
to show us how puny they are in the face
of everything they attempt to say.
And maybe that's why poets write,
to show the power of our powerlessness
in a storm at sea.

Roger Rosenblatt

I keep writing about the ordinary
because for me it's the home of the extraordinary.

Philip Levine

Contents

Acknowledgments

Many of these 'proems' appeared first in *The Christian Century*, and I bow first to poetry editor Jill Pelaez Baumgartner, who has had an inordinate number of my poems inflicted on her innocent and unsuspecting mailbox. Also my thanks to Paul Lake at *First Things*, Jessica Greenbaum at *Upstreet*, Cathy O'Connell-Cahill and Sarah Butler at *U.S. Catholic*, and Philip Harvey at *Eureka Street* in Australia. And to Barry Hudock at Liturgical Press, who had the brass and dash to ask me for a *second* book of proems even after he bravely published *A Shimmer of Something*. That man is nuts. And thanks especially to my friend Rachel Roscoe Lindberg for the very cool cover photograph, which is, as you might suspect, her headlong daughter. And thanks most of all to my subtle bride and our headlong children for the way they are poems of generosity and grace and wit and tenderness and humor and kindness and snickering. *I* get to live with *them* and therefore *I* am the luckiest blessedest man who ever lived. Fact.

That's the Kind of Brave You Wanted to Be

All I ever wanted to be when I was a little kid was a fireman.
I was a kid a long time ago when the word wasn't firefighters
Yet and there were no such beings as firewomen. All firemen
Were cool. They were quiet and friendly and strong. It didn't
Seem then that they were all young, perhaps because we were
Younger than they were. There were legends about the unreal
Food they ate and how they were all better chefs than the best
Chefs in the city. We used to talk quietly about how tough we
Would have to be to face a fire. Fires could roast you in a few
Seconds. You would be ashes and splinters of bone. Your dad
Could not even identify you. Even your teeth would be burnt.
Who could be that brave? Not to mention falling and carrying
Dead people and burning people and having walls fall on you.
Who could be that brave? Yet they were cheerful and friendly.
That's the kind of brave you wanted to be, the kind where not
Anything made you quail. Bullets were awful but a fire, man,
That was what hell was made of, fire was the sneer of Lucifer,
If a bullet hit you flat you wouldn't even know you were dead
But you would know every instant of pain when a fire ate you.
Yet they were efficient and affable and they played basketball
With us behind the firehouse. Today I get it that they were tall
Kids themselves, mostly. And most of them surely volunteers.
Who could be that kind of brave? One thing I know now, after
Many years of paying attention, is that there's a lot more brave
Than we know, or notice, or imagine. There's way more brave
Than craven. Sure, I know the evidence is everywhere against,
But you know I am right, and you know really great exemplars
Of why we're right, and there they are, in your local firehouse.

Astigmata

My lovely bride shows me her palms yesterday,
Holy Thursday, and indeed there are cuts on her
Palms, and she says cheerfully *These are paper-
Cuts from work but for an instant I wondered if
I had astigmata like Jesus*, and I started giggling
And couldn't hardly stop for a while, but then it
Hit me that the poor guy had the sharpest vision
Ever inflicted on a human being. What an awful
Relentless load that must have been, you know?
To see everything that would happen to you way
Into the future: that would be unmistakable hell.
It would. You know what I mean. Maybe he was
Seven years old when he had the first intimation,
When he had a vision clear as could be, of Pilate,
And the olivewood cross, and Malchus's ear wet
In the dust in the garden at night. Man—the poor
Kid, to *not* be astigmatic. You wish he had some
Days he forgot, maybe, or his buddies made him
Laugh so hard he could hardly stop; some weeks
When he was just a kid, a gawky sneery teenager,
A shy calm young guy everyone called Yeshuah!
As they ordered carpentered things from the shop.
They tease him as they leave and he is snickering
As he fills out the work order and then his future
Smashes in again on him. The poor guy. We wish
He did have days when he didn't see too well, am
I right? How weird to say that. But if he was truly
Us, which I think is the genius of the whole thing,

2

That he wasn't some superstar but an illuminated
Us, which means we're him and he's us somehow
In a way that means he didn't die, that he's a verb:
Then you feel for him. A young guy, hardly older
Than the soldiers blown up every day in our wars.
You wish he had a day sometimes when he didn't
See well, when he couldn't focus, when he forgot.

Holy Thursday

Friend of mine tells me this story, scratching his head
In an ancient gesture which means I know this is hard
To believe but I am just telling you what happened, &
I have no idea what it means either. It's after the Holy
Thursday service in the chapel, right after the Blessed
Sacrament has been paraded to the altar of repose and
Incensated, don't you love that word? Everyone sings,
And then some people stay all night praying. Keeping
Vigil, really, like the old days of Nocturnal Adoration.
So a few of us had decided to stay up all night praying
For a friend who is having it real hard. We figured this
Was as good a chance as any to do something together.
There's about ten other people in the church and seven
Of them leave after midnight. So there's four of us and
These other three folks. So along about three o'clock it
Isn't easy to stay awake—you *think* you can stay up all
Night but actually *doing* it is really hard—and the three
Other people are sound asleep, one of them snoring like
A horse, and my boys and I are dozing a little, and then
There's a ... stab of light in the air. Like a lightning bolt
That didn't shut off, you know what I mean? About six
Feet long and maybe two inches wide. It was just *there*.
Yes, everyone woke up. Nobody said anything. Wasn't
Hanging over the altar or anything. It was roughly eight
Feet above the pews. It wasn't buzzing or anything. Me,
I stood up to eye the fuse-box, thinking maybe something
Shorted out, but as soon as I stood up I knew to sit back
Down again. I can't explain any of this. We just sat and

Stared at it. You basically couldn't take your eyes off it.
After maybe seven minutes it vanished. One of my boys
Said later he thought it winked out like a light winks out
When you close a door. Like maybe someone left a door
Open and realized a few minutes later the door was open
And they shut the door quietly. So then it was dark again
With nothing but candles. Still, no one said anything. I'll
Always be happy that no one said anything. The first guy
Into the chapel at dawn was a young priest getting things
Ready for Good Friday service. He was happy to see lots
Of people, as he said, had spent the night in silent prayer.
We shook hands with him and said hello, but no one said
Anything about the stab of light. What's there to explain?
It just was there, is all I can say. What it means, or where
It came from, or who left the door open, I have no theory.
All I know is that there it was, and seven of us saw it, and
The snoring guy fell back asleep and snored like a grizzly
Bear the rest of the night. Me, I admire that guy. He snaps
Awake, sees what maybe is a miracle, and then goes right
Back to sleep. Got to get your beauty sleep, and maybe he
Sees miracles daily. Maybe that man has the right attitude,
You know? There are lots of miracles, but sleep's the best.

Your Theatrical Training

Most of what we learn when we are young is how to get by,
How to cruise, how to accomplish the required and not a jot
Or tittle more, how to fake it in every way, shape, and form,
How to pretend or hint toward interest while not being at all
Interested, how to seem to do one thing while doing another,
How to wear a mask, how to wear a mask under the mask in
Case of emergencies, how to say something you don't mean;
And this is not to even get into learning to smile and sneer at
Once, how to be present and absent, how to appear absorbed
While being the definition of unattached and inattentive. We
Learn such fakery, to be blunt. Why is that? We learn acting.
We are so gracefully false that a professional training is only
Returning consciously to adolescence, when you were seven
People at once, none of them speaking honestly to the others.
Do we ever really grow up? We inhabit so many selves. One
Role leads to another leads to eight more, and then cocktails.
Perhaps when we feel most unmoored we are most honest. It
Comes as a shock, being a rare thing. Unnerving and rattling.
You would do without it if you could. Maybe what we desire
When we talk about love is someone who cannot bear masks,
Theirs or ours. But are there such souls? Probably not. Some
People can get most of their masks off, though, and get down
To only two or three, and somehow the fact that they remove
Theirs gives you the awful urge to pry your own off. Careful;
That's best done in the dark, as we are all afraid of the mirror.

Poem Celebrating the Tiny Metal Flag-Holding Widget In the Shadows on the Stage of the Lovely Old Wooden Lincoln Theater in Pastoral Mount Vernon, Washington

To the right of the stage if you are facing it, as I am, sitting meditatively
In the dark, savoring the band, a wild Irish band, but I notice the stalwart
Little flag widget, huddled behind the banks of speakers, and off goes my
Mind into the bravura of flags, and how they cover any number of sins as
Well as courage and roaring grace, and how they have slept upon so very
Many coffins; but how they are also signs and symbols of communal pop
And verve and respect and debate and discourse and affection and humor,
And how they try to catch some insignia of a place and its tales; bemused
George Washington on state flag here, for instance, with his wry pageboy
Haircut like a Beatle on a bad hair day, or an intent beaver on the Oregon
Flag, or pelicans and eagles and bison and trees and adamant First People
On other American state flags. And who machined that little flag holder?
Who knelt to install it as he whistled something from Bruce Springsteen?
Who crafted it in some factory out by the old highway, and had a chicken
Sandwich for lunch, with a thermos of coffee his wife made for him? and
She left him a note, too, wrapped around a cookie, which makes him grin.
A state is a place where people who leave notes for each other live; a flag
Is a sign of such a place. So is a poem, in the end; a poem is a note pinned
To a public page. A poem is a wild letter from one citizen to all the others.
A poem says This is what I see and feel and sing—what do you folks sing?
Are we on the same page at all? Do we stand together under the same flag?

The Requisite Darkness

Lincoln was shot at about ten in the evening, years
Ago on Good Friday. Three men carried him down
A staircase, and across a street, and into a boarding
House. Imagine carrying a man six foot four across
A busy street. Did they have to wait for the traffic?
And what about the men who carried the other man
Into His tomb? This man was shorter, five foot four
Maybe, but He was bleeding too. Lincoln was taller
Than the bed in which they laid him. Neither stayed
Where he'd been put. How is a terrible death a good
Thing? Father Dennis said that His death was how it
All began, the resurrection, the hinge of history; that
Was *the requisite darkness*, he said. I remember how
He savored the words as he said them. He knew how
Eloquent they were. He nearly smacked his lips. But
Even then I knew he was blowing smoke. It's stupid.
It's the cause invented to fit the effect. The dead guy
Becomes a text on which to write a subsequent story.
But neither man fit easily into any story. Lincoln did
Save a nation but he caused a million people injuries
And death and loss and tears and rape and wounds of
Every kind. But he killed slavery. Yeshuah did speak
Words that will never be lost but very many millions
Of people have been murdered by those who claimed
To own His words. Each man the most awkward soul,
One gawky and somber and the other wry and mystic.
Each surely knowing his end all too well, all too early,
Each probably knowing years in advance they'd never

Grow old, never see grandchildren, never snatch a nap
Pleading an epic age. Neither man fit. Is that why they
Were murdered? Is that why we remember them now?
Do we have to murder our misfits so as to adore them?

The Song Sparrow

Walked out to the car this morning to find a small brown
Bird deceased on the windshield. A young song sparrow,
Neither naked gawky nestling nor chesty feathered elder;
A sort of a teenager, I guess. Cause of death not instantly
Evident, nor did I spend time determining its gender; no,
My brain got stuck on the teenager part. It's so fearsome,
Being a teenager. Everything is ten times louder. They're
Braver and stupider than any three older people; they *are*
Three people, most of the time. This is discombobulating
In the extreme. But we have no sympathy for them. We'd
Prefer to forget we were them; we deny that we ever were.
You know we do. If we wrote our histories we would skip
From twelve to twenty, from generally bucolic childhood,
At least fitfully, at least while finding refuge from trouble,
To beginner older idiocy, which itself takes a decade or so.
We get so impatient with teenagers. We want them to leap
Past stupid. But stupid is a great teacher, isn't it? Flailing
At least teaches you what alleys to avoid, if at all possible.
We have no mercy on them but they are in a thunderstorm,
And probably it seems like it will never end, and we whine
That they are wet yet again even after we advised as re wet.
And how wet we were too, brothers and sisters, how moist
And soaked and sopping and bedraggled we were, not even
Fully feathered at the time, trying to figure out how to soar,
And where to soar, and who, if anyone, would soar with us;
And if we were blessed we had parents, maybe parents who
Loved us even, but so often they just stood and sermonized
As we fell out of the nest, frightened and thrilled and lonely.

Goofing the Angel

The angels bring the news of the impossible yet again,
The same as usual. Just once you wish they would say
Something quotidian, something commonplace, a joke
About two rabbis, a ridiculous opinion about anything.
Do they never dicker about sports and literature where
They reside? Are they so shy about pride since Lucifer
That no one issues fatuous and fatuitous opinions? But
Such opinions are the engines of our daily bread, right?
We say things that are almost true—or slightly too true.
But the poor angels don't, or can't. I have always liked
Mary for her calm presence of mind when Gabriel shot
Into her afternoon and utterly screwed up the chore list;
And it's not at all irreverent to sometimes wonder, with
A smile, if she pondered goofing the angel for a minute,
Making him wait, asking him questions about wrestling
Or sparrows or pears or mercy as a marker of the divine.
She must have, you know? Remember how graceful she
Was, how accepting of the impossible. Or consider right
Afterward, when the shimmer that was the angel shivers
In the hot air like a song, and she is delighted and rattled
And wondering how exactly to explain this to old Joseph.
Surely she started giggling and could not cease, that such
A thing had happened to her, right here in the kitchen, by
The sink mortifyingly crammed with dishes. Old Gabriel,
She realizes, stood too close to the stove, and unwittingly
Carried some fish sauce back with him wherever he went;
And she starts snickering again, even as she feels the first
Kick of the child like a new idea, a fresh start, a first note.

11

Poem for My Friend Louis

By rights it would be a slim slender almost scrawny
Poem, and at least mention or refer to cross country
Running, and his childhood, and be poetic, but he is
Not typing here, so we will instead devote ourselves
To noting his essential courtesy, and his willingness
To laugh even though he is surprisingly melancholic
For a guy so willing to laugh. It's like he knows very
Well that he had better be willing to laugh, or else be
Stuck in a sort of pleasant sense of loss. I never knew
A man with such a ferocious memory for ebbed time;
It's the prime fuel of his own writing, even more than
Your men Proust or Joyce. Louis doesn't try to create
The world he lost again, like they did; he'd rather just
Sing it onto the page with a shy skill he'd never admit,
So that the reader too is 8 years old, in Massachusetts,
At Mass, or in the woods just as the snow starts again.
I don't know how he does it. You can see the first star
And the silent owl and the child with his chilled hands.
He'll hate this poem. It's too revealing. And he would
Never compare himself to Joyce and Proust. But I will,
As I am typing the poem, and Louis can go take a hike.
My conclusion is that he is a happier man than Marcel
Or James. They are famous, but both seem so very sad,
As if they were sentenced to life and never did recover;
Whereas Louis loves life so much he never can manage
To forget any of it. I think this is what makes him a tad
Melancholic; he knows when he goes, it will all go too,
And a storyteller cannot help but mourn the conclusion.

Sweeney's

Hauled an old longsleeved cotton shirt out of the drawer
Yesterday and once again time ground gears and shifted
Back forty years and this very shirt which was then more
Shirt than holes is handed to me by my lean gruff almost
Always quiet tall older brother who is of course my hero
And I gape at him unbelievingly and say Really, for *me?*
And he nods and so I come into possession of his college
Shirt earned playing football for a tavern or something as
Quotidian as that but not for me, not at all for me—that's
The point. Whatever we think is quotidian isn't. The pub
Was called Sweeney's. It closed long ago. I would not be
Surprised if this was the last Sweeney's shirt in existence.
I'll always have his shirt in a drawer. If I touch it, here he
Is in the room with me, smiling at how a shirt can make a
Kid speechless with astonished joy, even forty years later.
Isn't that amazing? We hardly ever say how amazing it is
That you can freeze time and reverse it and make it caper
And spin it back to anywhere anyone you used to be. Isn't
That amazing? A snatch of song, a scent, a battered collar,
A ratty old pub jersey. So many time machines. Yes, time
Wins. My brother withered and vanished. Yet here he sits
On the edge of the bed snickering at me as the shirt hangs
Way down past my knees. No religion owns resurrections.

Seamus

The way I discovered I had an older brother named Seamus
Was finding a photograph of him in the dank closet upstairs
Where no one went except us little brothers hiding out from
Each other playing games. Every family has this abandoned
Closet of arcana you think you might need but you never do.
I found an album of photographs. The cover was beautifully
Burnished wood. You hardly ever see a book with a wooden
Cover. It was the color of skin in summer. Inside was a baby
Over and over and over again; the same kid in every picture.
Who takes photographs every six minutes of the same child?
New parents do with their firstborn. I was fourteen years old.
I carried the book downstairs. My mother was in the kitchen.
Stew for dinner. The room redolent and yellow and the radio
Mumbling on its yellow shelf. All my years I will remember
How my mom didn't say a word; she stared and turned away.
She didn't burst into tears or hug me or anything; the fraught
Instants just slide past at the same speed as the other instants.
I suppose mom was not the hugging type of mom or the type
To burst into tears, either; she still is bone and grin and glare,
Someone who has seen everything but doesn't wail or blame.
A little later she told me who he was, their first baby, Sudden
Infant Death Syndrome. That means No One Knows. He was
There and then he wasn't. Soon after these photographs. You
Can understand how you would have to try to put all the pain
In a book and close the book and put it in the closet where no
One goes. You could understand that. Your father talks to his

First son every day. *He went on ahead,* is what dad says now.
We all talk about him now that the book opened; when we're
All at the table I look around when someone speaks his name.

At Marine Park by Flatbush Avenue, August 1974

One time my friends and I were playing in a basketball game
In Brooklyn. This was a summer league game, a windy night
Near the beach. An old man had swept shards of glass before
We straggled out to warm up. We were pretty good and were
Up by eight at halftime. The other team had two fine players,
Though, one guy a classic silent workhorse and the other guy
Unreal talented but chippy and showy. Twice he lost the ball
On stupid plays and twice he glared at a teammate like it was
The teammate's fault, which it wasn't. Everyone on the court
Knows what's happening on the court, by the way. *We* know.
Mostly if another team is tense among themselves, you savor
It as another tool in the box. Sometimes, though, you feel bad
For the other guys having to put up with a diva, and you close
Down the diva just because, or deliberately hit him in the face
With a pass. It's like for a minute you want to say to the other
Team, hey, brothers, sorry you have to put up with such a tool.
This game was like that. We put our best defender on the dork,
And we were cruising to a win by maybe ten points, enough to
Claim the game but not hammer the point, when the older man
Who had swept up calls time out. This is summer league, when
Rules are relaxed, so the ref calls time, and the guy steps out to
Sweep up a little sand or something, and he chats with our best
Defender, who tells us that the man told him to hack the starlet.
Turns out the kid with all the moves is his son, and he wants to
Make the kid learn to work harder, even when things fall apart;
Especially when stuff falls apart. The old guy *apologized* to me,
Said our teammate. He said he was sorry to ask me to be unfair,
But he wanted to give the kid a chance to be more than talented.

He says he talked to the ref also. So that's how we played those
Last five minutes, hammering the kid at every turn. We took off
The second the game ended, not wanting to get into it with other
Guys, but even now, once in a while, on a breezy summer night,
I remember that game, and the intent father, and his huge broom.
I wish I could remember if the kid took his punishment stoically,
But all I remember is staring at his teammates to see if they were
Going to make a stand for their guy. It's telling that they did not.

A Chicago Story

I knew a cop once when I lived in Chicago who was
A gifted storyteller and he told me a hundred stories
About chasing thugs and breaking up gangs and pub
Brawls and one time catching a guy who stole lamps
From chapels, how weird is *that* for a criminal focus,
As he said; but once when I asked the single moment
That came to mind first in his career, he told this tale:
One day we go to get a guy who's been kiting checks.
This is where you float a check and surf on the credit
That the bank gives you because they think you made
A deposit. An old trick. We knock on the door and he
Answers it and he knows what's up, you could tell on
His face. Just then a kid jumps between us. The kid is
Maybe nine years old max, and he cocks his fists, and
Says, I kid you not, *you want him, you go through me*.
I can see it today, the way the boy has his fists cocked
Exactly like boxing photos. The boy is maybe seventy
Pounds of brave, you know? I mean, we worked it out,
And nobody got hurt, and it ended as good as could be
Expected, given the scenario, but that defiant kid, man,
I will always remember that kid. He was really serious.
He was ready to go to war for his dad, and the dad was
Basically a slimer. This kid is maybe four feet high but
He's ready to rock, he was going to protect and defend
No matter what the odds. I mean, it's funny but it isn't,
You know? Kid was crazy brave. I'll always remember
That kid. The way he just jumped in there. Crazy brave.

A Bride with Brass

Today's remarkable vision: a woman in her bridal dress
Walking purposefully along the street. This was enough
Of an amazing sight by itself, but the determined stride,
The intent look, her *I am going someplace, and I am not*
Worrying about how I look, even though I know you are
All looking, attitude—that got me. I mean, of course you
Wonder where she was going, and where she came from,
And why she is alone, and if this is a just little aberrance
In an otherwise tightly plotted day, or if she was hustling
To catch the bus, and where is the entourage you usually
See flanking a bride, the cheerful best friends, the joyous
But slightly jealous sisters although they would never say
Such a thing even to each other after a few bottles of beer
At the reception, or even perhaps the groom, where is he?
I was caught in traffic and sped right along and only later
Did I think should I have stopped, and offered her a ride?
I mean, what if she was hustling to the actual ceremony?
What if her Ford broke down and the groom was forlorn?
But I have a lovely bride of my own, and I am on the one
Bride per groom plan, which I renew every morning with
A deep and amazed glee, so I hope the bride on the street
Made it to wherever it was she was headed, or whomever.
The whomever is a lucky soul, seems to me—a bride who
Has the panache to stroll along unconcernedly even as she
Knows full well folks are gaping; that's a bride with brass.

Poem on Our 28th Wedding Anniversary

The first time the woman who would be my wife kissed me, we
Were just talking idly but interestedly, you know how that goes,
There's no agenda but you are just interested, for no reason you
Could name; I mean, she was beautiful and shapely and riveting
And all that, but I swear I wasn't angling or making a play at all.
We were just chatting easily, standing on the sidewalk. This was
In Boston, in an old Irish neighborhood. It was a spring evening.
Sometimes I try as hard as I can to remember if there were birds:
First owls, early nighthawks, a brace of night herons. I suppose I
Want to remember exactly everything. That was the last moment
I didn't have her in my mind all the time. I leaned in and she sort
Of leaned up and we kissed and then it was after. Just like that, it
Was after, when a moment before it had been before. Do we ever
Gape enough at this sort of thing? And it happens all the time, all
Over the world. Well, not *everyone* is suddenly leaning in, for no
Reason that he could ever articulate, and kissing my tender bride,
Let's not go *that* far, but *I* did, and she let me, and she was *eager*,
I think, or else just so shocked that she didn't get her heat shields
Into the upright and locked position quick enough; even she does
Not know which. So neither of us know why we leaned in and up,
Which I have always liked. To be startled and delighted and then
Realize very soon afterward that now you are in after, whereas an
Instant ago you were in before; it still gives me the happy shivers.

Summer Camp

A kid asks me if I ever went to summer camp and I start laughing
And he says *what?* and I explain that I was inflicted upon the Boy
Scouts of America summer camp in the mountains of remote high
New York State which is actually unbelievably rural and beautiful
Much more so than you think when they hear the words *New York*,
Words that probably make you think of pigeons and gangsters and
Fifth Avenue and delicatessens and corruption. But Upstate! child,
I say, for many years I told stories of my misadventures as a Scout,
And for many years I snickered about all the skills I was terrible at,
Like swimming and knots and cooking and orienteering and hiking
And making fires and erecting tents and pretty much everything we
Were supposed to do and earned merit badges for—but no one ever
Enjoyed Boy Scout Camp more than me. The wild light on the lake,
The footprints of deer and raccoon and mink, the rotating red-tailed
Hawks screwing the sky closer to the earth, the seethe of hot breeze
Through the trees my brother Peter had taught me to see: hemlocks,
Pines, walnut, birch and beech, ash and alder, cottonwoods, locusts,
Spruce and willow, oaks and elms, even once a big portly basswood.
I suppose I began to learn some languages there, is one way to say it.
There were guys then who ragged the Scouts as geeks, as militaristic
Chumps, but my experience was that the Scouts were another species
Of clan and tribe and club and gang, with the added plus, huge to me,
Of two weeks deep in forests that were once the lands of the Lenape.
To be fifteen years old and sitting in a clearing and start to get it that
The woods were a calm story, and the mountains were a tall story, &
The red-tailed hawk conducting recon was a sharp story, and the jays
Stealing potato chips were headlong riveting amazing devious stories:
I adored summer camp, though I never did earn even one merit badge.

Flew

One time when my twin sons were eight years old
And on their first league basketball team there was
A boy on the other team who was small but as fast
As could be although not yet in command of a ball
And his arrow of a body at the same time. This kid
Takes off at one point from a standing start and his
Launch was so sudden and forceful that both shoes
Stayed behind. He no kidding flew out of his shoes.
A few of us parents saw this and started snickering,
And then a boy on our team, a gentle and solicitous
Lad named Michael, picked up the sneakers and ran
After the speedster, who by now was sliding around
Helplessly on the buffed shining floor, and Michael
Was pursuing him around picks and screens waving
The shoes, and the ref is laughing so hard he cannot
Blow his whistle, and us parents are totally losing it,
And even the most intent boys on both teams finally
Stop and laugh, and the falcon boy giggles and steps
Back into his sneakers, and time rolls on, snickering
A little maybe, but you know what I remember most
This morning, other than the lovely fact that the bolt
Of a boy was thankfully not embarrassed? His shoes,
Sitting there astonished at so amazingly being empty.
There were seven seconds there outside the narrative,
You know what I mean? When a thing just happened
That just doesn't happen. There's some wisdom here
About what humor is and why something is amusing,
But there's also something deep about grace and gift

And attentiveness and never assuming anything at all.
Also perhaps there's something to be said about laces
Being double-knotted, or some fatherly coachly thing
Like that. But stay with me for a minute in the instant
When the shoes sat there suddenly startled and lonely.

Down by Fulton Fish Market

I graduated from college in May and started looking for jobs
A week later but no jobs were looking for me. I was worried
About coins so I did not ride the subway but instead plodded
From the Battery all the way to 155th Street and east to west,
Including both Upper Sides of Central Park. I tried museums,
Newspapers, publishing houses, magazines, history societies,
Ten libraries, jazz clubs, and even once a sailors' benevolent
Society, down by Fulton Fish Market. That interview trickles
Back into my memory this morning, redolent and mysterious,
For the interviewer understood that there was no work for me,
Nor would I have been qualified for whatever work might've
Been available, but that I was weary and frightened and bleak,
And he poured a cup of the darkest densest coffee and invited
Me to talk about ships and the sea and stories and what labors
I ultimately had in mind if I was going to do work that I loved.
We sat there for two hours easy chatting about Joshua Slocum
And Captain James Cook, and Jack London, and various ships
I had seen for myself, like the whaler *Charles W. Morgan*, and
Ships on which he had served, both mercantile and U.S. Naval,
And I bubbled on and on about Stevenson and Kipling and C.S.
Forester and how my plan was to work for newspapers because
What could conceivably be cooler than reporting in New York?
And while working on newspapers, eventually as the editor, I'd
Write books on the side, and essays too of course, and here and
There perhaps a poem, so that someday I'd have a slim volume
Of poems to my name, wouldn't that be cool, because everyone
Should commit a slim volume of poems, don't you think? Even
Now I can see his face, wrinkled and amused and sort of kindly

In a ragged way—*hewn* is a good word. I was too self-absorbed
Then to turn myself off and listen to him, a far more fascinating
Man, but I think now that I learned a great deal from him: grace,
Patience, empathy, kindness, listening, humility, the way an ear
Can be an oar to someone who has been drifting dark and lonely.

The Morning Bus

The schoolbus croaks down our hill at just exactly the right time
Again which is constantly amazing to me—how *does* that driver
Persuade that bright groaning whale of a thing along so deftly so
Bouncingly saggingly cheerfully and never is he off by a minute,
Never that I remember in twenty years? Now that our kids aren't
On the bus, I watch for it even more closely, for reasons I cannot
Quite explain—the easy words would be sentiment and nostalgia
And memory and a silent sadness that their littleness is now gone
Forever, and those were swift and hilarious and tumultuous years,
Yes they were, with an incredible amount of mud and yelling and
Sandwiches and laundry and *more* sandwiches, my God, how can
Three children eat a thousand sandwiches a day, how can that *be*?
But the inchoate desire is some sort or shape or song of reverence,
I think—something about witness and celebration, and memory as
A lever for the present joy; you cannot wallow in the past, but you
Sure can use it as a staircase. Something like that. So I am present
In the kitchen window at 8:29 exactly if at all possible, to be given
The gift of a kid licking the window, or a kid waving at me, or one
Little kid this morning inarguably and thoroughly picking his nose.
You wouldn't think in the usual course of things that a boy picking
His nose would be a glorious and poignant and thrilling and joyous
Sight, something that seemed truly and deeply holy, but it sure was,
To me. All children are my children and yours and the bus bounces
Down the street every morning and we are not dead and all is grace.

On Halsted Street

One time years ago I was playing basketball in Chicago
At a battered playground court when a guy on the other
Team came down awkwardly and crumpled to the court
And screamed; he had torn apart his knee so thoroughly
That it was bent in a way knees do not go. One guy said
Later he had heard it tear, a terrible gentle savage sound.
Most of us had to turn away—you couldn't bear to look;
One guy walked off into the bushes and threw up, it was
That awful. But one guy took his shirt off and bent down
And tucked it under the broken guy's neck, like a pillow.
I remember that. A tiny thing, I guess. But not tiny at all.

Lily

The kindergarten bus bounces past me this morning as
I shamble out to my car and a little cheerful kid waves
To me shyly and whatever it is we are way down deep
Opens like a fist that's been clenched so long it did not
Think it would ever open again and for a moment I am
That kid and she is my daughter and I'm waving to her
Hoping she will wave to me and we think that we can't
Write that for which we do not have words but actually
Sometimes you can if you go gently between the words

Poem for Father's Day

No one talks about this, but every dad who ever had a son
Had and loved this moment, during which he and his boy,
About age two, stand in the woods or at the beach, or even
In God help us the bathroom, and the father says, son, first
Rule is don't wet yourself. All production is out and about.
After that you want to try for accuracy if possible, but only
Sometimes does that matter. Just as in basketball, footwork
Is key. Never pee on your own feet. Some idiot friend will
Someday tell you that you can toughen your feet by peeing
On them. This is a canard. When you are sure you are done,
Close up shop. Never leave the door open. Think of it all as
Returning water to the generous earth; we are mostly water,
And water runs through us, and we should be grateful for it
More than we generally are, even during times like this that
Seem pedestrian. But there is no such entity as a pedestrian
Moment, only moments in which we have not looked close
Enough for the huge thing hiding behind the ostensible tiny.
Questions? No? Then, son, let's zip up and get back to base.

Poem for the Wooden Shutters and Little Mesh Grilles in Old Confessional Booths

Which you hardly ever see anymore, which is a shame,
Because they beautifully allowed you to be a bit hidden
As you poured your heart out. Psychologically brilliant.
And there was pace and rhythm and theater to the thing,
A cadence, a concatenation, really and truly a narrative.
I came to enjoy it very much. The rustle of your curtain,
Alerting Father to your arrival. A courteous pause as he
Gave you time to get settled and remember the opening
Bars of the song: *Bless me Father for I have sinned it's*
And etc. Then he opened the shutter. Pine, oak, walnut?
Someone cut and carved it, of course. Someone worked
For hours to get that plank of wood exactly right for that
Exact use. Then you could dimly see the other's outline.
Father might have a tiny light on in his half of the booth
So that, between sinners, he might read the Racing Form.
You opened with *Bless me Father*, and he assented to do
So, his hand floating slowly and steadily. His aftershave
Was prevalent. You spoke or chanted or blurted out your
Sins of commission or omission. A good and wise priest
Would listen most carefully for what you weren't saying.
As I recall there was rarely any discussion of any details.
The whole point of the thing, and a surpassingly brilliant
Thing it is, is that you are, in private, without substantive
Penalty or punishment, or recrimination or incarceration,
Unburdening yourself, being searingly honest about what
You have been awful at, done badly, done to the innocent,

30

Done with malice aforethought; you are straight about not
Being straight. The priest does not then assume or absolve
Your sins; he cannot eat your sins, take them into himself
As did the mysterious Christ; but he can be witness, stand
As interlocutor, bridge, sentinel between lies and honesty;
And in that role he can then convey that you *are* absolved,
If you are in truth seeking absolution. Does everyone who
Confesses tell the whole truth? Nope. Do people lie? Sure.
But it is not a court. It is a chance to admit you have acted
In ways you know yourself to be low and mean and slimy.
When I was a boy I skipped out of confession delighted at
The paucity of the penalty; as a man, I walk out moved by
The ancient genius of murmured unburdening and witness;
But I do miss the quiet shadowed booth, the intricate mesh
Of the window grille, the soft rattle of the shutter, Father's
Aqua Velva, the rustle of the Racing Form, the warm dark.

Rules for Being an Altar Boy at Saint John Vianney Parish for the Liturgical Year 1964

If you have to sneeze on the altar do so quietly and turn
Your head away from the Holy Sacrament. Please carry
A handkerchief in the pocket of your trousers. No jeans.
Wear good shoes. No sneakers. Arrive 30 minutes early
Minimum: 5 minutes early is 25 minutes late. The bells,
As a crucial part of the Mass, are rung firmly but gently.
It is the unaware altar server who rings them too loudly.
Be attentive. You too are an integral aspect of the Mass.
You are witnessing and abetting a miracle. Always treat
The Mass that way. Your service allows the miraculous
Easier passage into this plane. Never let your cassock be
Stained or sullied. Similarly your surplice. Do not under
Any circumstances drink the wine or eat the consecrated
Hosts. You will be tempted to do so. Resist the Tempter.
You may be late for, or fail to appear for, only one Mass.
If you are late for or miss a second Mass, your privileges
Are suspended. Two boys in nine years have been ousted.
Don't become the third. Honor the parents who are proud
Of their son and his service as witness to Holy Sacrament.
It is a gift to serve on the altar. Treat your service as a gift.
Listen to the Holy Spirit as you serve. The Mass is ancient
And comes to us directly from the hand and words of God
When he assumed human form in the person of the Christ.
In and through and suffusing every aspect of the quotidian
Is the sacred. Treat Father with respect, but be aware of his
Own complex humanity. The Sacristy is not a locker room:

There is no horseplay, no vulgar language, and no shouting.
If you have a problem, or a question, of any sort, or if there
Is anything whatsoever that you wish to speak to me about,
Be assured that I will keep it in confidence, and listen with
Respect for your own miraculous existence, and admirable
Service to the Church Eternal and particularly to our parish.
Finally as to the length of the hair, any length is acceptable,
As long as the hair is noticeably clean. Christ had long hair,
But you can be sure that His was clean. Boys—be like Him.

Such Delicious Absence

Given the unimaginably huge number of things that can go wrong,
And often do, and seem to sometimes go wrong in raging bunches,
Long steadily drumming runs of wrong, bursts of bad luck and bad
Fortune and accidents and illnesses and misunderstandings and ten
Mistakes caused by hurriedly trying to address the last eight things
That went wrong, isn't it incredible when just for a minute nothing
Goes wrong? Or a whole day? One whole day when you didn't say
That's not what I meant, or *my bad*, or *I apologize*, or *overdraft?!?*
Or *how long have you had that cough?* Or *another new manifold?!*
Or anything of that sort or import. We train ourselves to play loose
Defense all the time, to patrol the perimeter, to calmly expect news
That will not be thrilling. You know when the phone rings at three
In the morning it won't be with good news. Yet whole hours go by,
Whole days, bursts of days, maybe a week, when wrong goes right
Past like it caught the wrong bus and isn't paying close attention to
The address. It will be back, sure it will; it never *stays* lost—but we
Should maybe mark and sing and savor and relish and revel in such
Delicious absence more than we do. I mean, I am the worst as to all
This, to me the absence of trouble only means it's growing stronger
Somewhere, and picking up speed; but maybe I am a fool and when
Nothing is going wrong that's what's supposed to happen. Maybe it
Is the case that we invented religions to personify just these matters;
The hell of a parade of things going wrong, and the heaven of none.

Learning Owl

When our children were little there were owls
Out back in the fir and cedar trees every night
From dusk almost to dawn; believe me I knew
Their hours as for various reasons we were all
Up at all of those hours at one time or another.
So deep in the nether reaches one night I'm up
With a small boy and we hear the owls rooling
And hoolering and hewhewing as the boy says.
Those are excellent words, I say. I never heard
Those words before in the world. I learned owl,
He says sleepily. I listened good. They go slow
If you ask politely. I think they feel bad that we
Are trapped in the cage of the house. They chat
All night, you know. I wonder where their dads
Live and if their dads tuck them in like you do?

Poem in Which I Am Sitting
At the Sullivan Square Station
On the Orange Line in Boston
Staring at the Old Schrafft's
Candy Factory, and Contemplating
The Rubble and Smash of an Affair
With a Young Lady That Has Slumped
From Bad to Worse to Epically Awful,
And Realizing That Even as I Am Idly
Pondering the Detritus of This Terrible
Affair I Am Much More Interested in
The History of the Old Candy Factory
Than I Am in the Young Lady, Which
Probably Explains, Very Well Indeed,
Why the Affair Is Disastrous, as I Am
Not in Love With Her at All in the Least,
Which I Realize Just as the Train Arrives

Well, the title of this poem pretty much says it all.

Warming Up

Curiously what I always loved best about playing soccer
In high school was not at all the games which were grim
And tense more often than enjoyable even when we won
Which was a relief rather than a triumph; it was warming
Up beforehand. The sprawl of the ridged and pitted grass,
The easy pairing-off for lazy passes back and forth, spray
Spinning off the ball as it whizzed along through the dew;
The game was only really a game before the whistle blew.

The Tender Next Minute

One time when we were kids my two younger brothers
And I were absorbed with ropes and climbing and what
Heights could be scaled by intrepid adventurers like us,
So we scaled the garage, and then we scaled a massive
Sweetgum, and then we tried to scale a neighbor's shed
But he glared and roared and we escaped into the hedge
Riven with tunnels and lairs that only we knew, and it's
That moment in the lurk of the hedge that I want to sing
Here for a moment. We huddled, panting, at the second
Turn, under the iglooish canopy of the forsythia bushes.
I had the rope, and my next brother had our kid brother,
Actually holding him by the hand, and we were smiling
And thrilled and frightened and sunlight rippled through
The tiny yellow flowers of the bushes and not far away
A robin inquired as to just *what* was all this hullabaloo?
You were there too, remember, in *your* childhood cave,
The moist soil, the laboring beetles, the unwritten poem
Of the lost leaves, the duff, the thin spidery bones of old
Twigs. Once in a while we all stopped sprinting and just
Stared at what was there all around us, the wealth of dirt,
The sudden green feather about to adorn its second wild
Animal, the tender next minute waiting for us to emerge.

What People Gave Me One Evening
In Rural Coastal Oregon after I Told
Them Stories in a Lovely Tiny Library

A stack of brownies as big as bricks for my children.
A small paper bowl of red and orange salmonberries.
An antler from a spike buck, perhaps three years old,
Perhaps a black-tailed deer, perhaps now gargantuan.
Cranberry syrup made up the coast about eight miles.
Handshakes of all sorts. A photograph; their one son,
Just deceased; *we just thought that you should have it.*
Blackberry jam, homemade. Honey, homemade. Salal
Sprigs, elderberry sprigs. Canned smoked salmon and
Tuna, caught about two miles to the west of where we
Stood in the library. A baby girl hoisted up so she and
I could look each other in the eye. She sneezed. Books
To scrawl upon. Huckleberry leaves. A cougar's tooth,
Gleaming. A man gripped me by the shoulder and said
Nothing. His was a remarkably expressive grip. People
Give you things without any things in their hands. You
Know what I mean. They are eloquent without needing
To speak. We hardly ever talk about this. I shuffled off
With my arms full. I had been slathered by the glorious
And only a little of it was in the basket I tucked into my
Car. People were hungry for something. I knew what it
Was and it wasn't me; but I could tell stories that could
Point to what it is we are all starving for. We work and
Yearn and struggle and dream for it. Occasionally when
We gather together, if there is humility, if there is story,
If there is honesty, then there is plenty of food for us all.

Poem for the Tall Man Who Interrupted Me Last Night During a Reading to Say That He Didn't Much Care for What I Was Reading and Could I Read My Better Stuff?

An excellent question, to which I could only say yes, cautiously,
Trying to answer the actual question; but then comes the morass,
During which we have to try to calculate which is the better wine.
Is that which is humorous better than that which is somber? What
About stories about other people, are they inherently better than a
Story about myself? Are the best stories about me about everyone
Else, and that's why they are good? You see the puzzle, sir, I said,
And then I maundered and stumbled and mumbled and ambled on,
Keeping an eye on him to see if he would get up and walk out, but
Also well aware that everyone else had their own opinion on good
And bad. The stories that made people weep, that hit people where
They live behind their dignity, that hit home in their hearts, I think
Those are the better songs, because they crack something and open
Something else, let something out that doesn't get out much. Tales
That make people laugh also seem glorious to me; no one gets hurt
While laughing, and there's no violence or lies or theft or extortion,
Which seems like an admirable and rare state of affairs. Tough pick,
Tears or laughter; which is why I shoot for both, and then slip away,
Hoping that at least some people were rattled and entertained, if not
The tall guy. He didn't leave, though; I figured that was a good sign.

Poem in Which My Wife Spoons Her Mother's Ashes from a Soulless Metal Box to the Beloved Old Blue Cookie Jar

At her mother's express instructions, I hasten to add.
Except none of the family has gotten around to doing
The actual act. So the youngest child of the deceased
Sits down at the dining room table to do it. How does
One spoon your mother from a box into a cookie jar?
Slowly, reverently, absorbedly. You don't want to be
Spilling your mom. There are all sorts of details here,
Like the blue cloth she spread out, and the holy water,
And the prayers, and the gentle humor of the moment,
And the way her mama herself would have giggled at
The odd of it all, and then the two of them would have
Started laughing so hard they couldn't stop and a little
Ash would have spilled, and they would probably just
Scoop it back up with a spatula, and swear not to ever
Tell *anyone* cross your heart, which would have made
Them start giggling helplessly again, but let's not have
Time for the details this morning. Let's just pause with
The two of them laughing so hard their cheeks actually
Are sore for days afterward; that's a good place to stop.

Once in a While We Should Say What Is

I was pawing through a shelf of books the other day
When out fell a note from my late brother in his tiny
Adamant wry inarguable crisp half-cursive-half-not
Handwriting, and just for an instant I saw and heard
Him at his desk, in his study, his mustache bristling,
Black coffee half-cold, the burl of his body wrapped
In the arms of the chair that held him for thirty years,
A chair as big as a horse and twice as heavy. I *heard*
Him, I tell you, I did, and I *saw* him, half-shadowed,
Scribbling notes: his philatelic pursuits, notes for his
Class next week, notes on a book he was going to do
About Benedictine spirituality . . . then I was only me
By the bookshelf again. But for a second I was in my
Brother's study, watching him. It was late, everybody
Was in bed, but not him, as usual he was up late with
Coffee. He was wearing a sweater. The scritch of his
Pen. His shoulders like boulders. The dim procession
Of his books, organized by genre and author. He died
Three years ago. But I *saw* him, absorbed, thoroughly
Attentive, scrawling notes. There's way more possible
Than we think possible; possible turns out to be a verb.
I don't know how else to explain things like this. They
Happen all the time to all of us and we hesitate to gape
About them publicly because the words sound like pap,
Miracle and *epiphany* and *vision*, you come off as nuts,
A religious goober who talks to owls and addled saints.
But you know and I know that this happens. I guess we
Will always understandably be hesitant to chat about it,

42

Which is fine, as no one enjoys being labeled a goober;
But once in a while, like here, we should admit that it's
Real, and it happens all the time, and it's scary and cool.
That's all. Once in a while we should gently say what is.

In the Sacristy Just before the Dawn Mass

The first time I served Mass on my own I had just turned ten
Years old and thought myself a whole different order of boy,
Being so old. The kid assigned to be my partner didn't show.
If I was merciful I would not name him. His name was Frank
Torricello. He just slept in, although he insisted later that it'd
Been a family emergency—*More like a pillow emergency*, as
Father Whelan observed, chortling. He sat me down and gave
Me a pep talk. You know what to do, you have done it before,
Now you just calmly combine his job and yours, he said. I get
It that you are a little nervous. I get shaky every time I step on
The altar, you know. What if I forget something, or mangle it?
Can you imagine Mrs Deedy's face if I screwed up the liturgy?
She'd be on the phone with the bishop so fast your head would
Spin and mine would be on the chopping block. I'll tell you my
Trick. I move real slowly on purpose. I pretend I'm underwater.
That sounds weird, I know, but it works, and it also looks great,
Like we are alert to the ancient rhythms of the rite, before there
Was television, before people hurried so much. I start out really
Slow and then your instinct and training take over. Also I recall
That a Mass is stories, a miracle, and a meal, in that exact order,
And even I can remember that trinity. If *I* can serve a Mass, you
Sure can, because *you* are a bright young man and *I* am an idiot.
But I am an ordained idiot, the bishop trusts me, and I trust you,
So here we go, you go first, remember we are underwater . . . Go!

Pop

Here's a moment. I am sitting with my dad
In his yard on Florida. He is 94 *and change*,
As he says. We are sitting silently, listening
To the birds. The vegetation is, well, *riotous*,
As Pop says, always a student of good words.
Then a tiny lizard takes it into his or her head
To climb aboard the paternal ship and ascend
His left leg. Pop doesn't move or say a word.
The lizard makes it over the equator and then
Up dad's left arm. Pop says quietly *he prefers*
The west face, maybe the easier line of ascent.
Finally the lizard gets up to Mount Rushmore,
But something spooks him, and he leaps away
Into the bushes, and Pop grins and says *rarely*
Have I been graced by such an ambitious soul.
This pretty much sums up Pop. Calm, patient,
Attentive, unflappable, interested in all shapes
And manners of life—and always the bon mot.
Anyone else would have shrieked, but Pop was
Genuinely sorry that he and his climber did not
Get a chance to look each other in the eye from
The most intimate of vantage points. A minute
Later we went in to lunch, slowly and carefully.

The Usual Perfect Mask

I got to talking to a young woman the other day
In the course of the social ramble—she was my
Driver from one place to another, about sixteen
Minutes, and I'd never see her again, so I asked
About her life, trying to be polite, and she spoke
About her little boy, age three, a totally cool kid,
And with pleasure she told stories about the boy,
Funny stuff he'd said, his best recent adventures,
And then I asked about his father, and she began
To weep. You know how you can tell someone's
Crying because they don't talk when they should
Be talking? It was like that. We . . . are divorcing,
She said after a minute. Or properly he is leaving
Me, which means I won't see my son every night.
That's why I am crying. I can't bear that thought.
I can't bear that. I read to him at night. We crawl
Into his bed with ten books and read them slowly.
Sometimes they are all orange or green or purple.
I'm sorry. I shouldn't cry. Well, here we are. The
Blue door there to the left, just go in there and Ed
Will take care of you, and I climbed out and there
Was Ed and she drove away and for the millionth
Time I thought about how often if you ask people
Gently to open windows, they do, and their selves
Pour out, startled and shy and shocked and crying
And for a moment without the usual perfect mask.

Poem for My Friend Lee

It was your dignity that struck me first and most,
Especially as you were about as tall as a sparrow;
And then your cheerful calm grace, and courtesy.
Grace under duress, that's the best story of us all,
Of course, but a genuine easy unforced unwitting
Courtesy is just a delicious and alluring character
Flag, it seems to me. You were always fascinated
By everyone else—which I think is why everyone
Else was quickly fascinated by you. Also the size-
Of-a-bird thing, that was interesting. How could a
Woman of such parts be only the size of a smile?

Basketball Dads

In the grocery store the other day, right by the beets,
A guy about my age turns and looks at me twice and
Says hey! and I look at him more closely and realize
He and I are former basketball dads. For about seven
Years I saw this man twice a week during the season,
And we must have spent a hundred hours standing in
Gymnasiums all over the city, chatting idly about this
And that, and now for the life of me I cannot retrieve
His name from the vault. It's a nickname, I know that.
The second in which I would say *hey Tom* or *hey Jim*
Passes, and I retreat to Guytalk, in which you can say
Hey or *hey man* or *dude* or *what's up* and it's all legit,
No guy ever gets offended if you don't use his name —
It's almost like all men have the same first name, in a
Pinch. I mean, in the end, you can call all men *man* &
You would get by swimmingly. We chatted idly about
Our sons for a minute, and then he went for rutabagas
And I went for avocados. On the way home I pondered
This whole male name-no-name thing for a little while,
But then I grew sad about how time is so inarguable &
Irretrievable, even if you try as hard as you can to take
Copious notes and jot down every tiny-not-tiny instant,
As I do. But then you meet a guy by the beets, and you
Remember not his name but the fact that those cheerful
Echoing gyms crammed with gangly shrieking giggling
Boys are long ago and far away. Mostly we forge ahead
When we are forcibly reminded that so much is so gone,

What choice do we have, right? But sometimes you just
Sit in your car and try not to cry. Some days I notice lots
Of folks just sitting in their cars, and I think I know why.

Poem for My Friend John Roscoe

Listen, there are a lot of reasons to like and admire
My friend John, foremost among them the fact that
He's the most gentle unassuming gracious guy you
Could ever meet, the kind of man who obviously is
Hiding some deeper weird or angry, but it turns out
He's not, he really genuinely is gracious and gentle,
Even though he got hammered in life in such a way
That he ought to be a seething simmering explosion
Waiting to happen, a volcano of a man. But he isn't.
This knocks me out. It's like he told his own rage to
Piss off and leave him alone. I mean, who *does* that?
He channels his love into his two wild glorious kids,
I see that, and he makes a point of digging everyone
Else, and he drinks in his vast clan like the best beer,
And you never met a guy more absorbed by the holy
Green craggy furred feathered watery miracle world,
But still, it's the telling his own rage off that gets me.
Perhaps he punches his pillow at night, or punts a cat
Here and there on principle, but I doubt it. Somehow
He found a way to mail rage elsewhere. That's a hell
Of a great idea, isn't it? Maybe that's how the future
Arrives; maybe that's the *only* way the future arrives.

A Tenderness in the World

My brother calls and tells me that our dad has fallen
Several times recently and that I should be prepared.
I know what he means and I say thanks but then I sit
And ponder the word *prepared* for a while. Prepared
For no dad? But the man is a tree, a gentle statement
Of insistence on grace and dignity, a lean tenderness
In the world. He's who you call when you have good
News. He's always genuinely happy and proud. He is
Wry and honest and wise. He never gives you advice
Unless you ask specifically for it. This is rare; almost
Everyone else, myself included, inflicts advice all too
Freely, which undercuts whatever wisdom might hide
There, huddled under the withering hot gob of the ego.
Not Pop, though. He just sits there smiling gently, and
You ask quietly, and he says something quietly, and if
You are me, you go sit alone a while and chew it slow.
There's always more there than there seems to be; this
Is also a pithy explanation of the man himself. An oak,
A serenity, an avatar of gentle. I know him—he'll slip
Off stage without ado. Probably in his sleep. So as not
To bother our mom. She'll wake up first and she'll see
The way his face says something only she could know.

Ten Thousand Smiles

I was just calculating that my sister,
Whom I have known for 700 months,
Which is nearly three thousand weeks,
Which is nearly twenty thousand days
(which is a remarkable number of days
When you think about it; I mean, that's
A stunning heap of pain and laughter),
Has smiled at me roughly 10,000 times,
Give or take a few thousand. Now, did
She also occasionally snarl and shriek?
O yes she did. But *ten thousand smiles*,
That's a remarkable number of smiles,
And I want to stay with the smiles here.
Q: what are the cumulative effects of so
Many smiles? Can you get smile burns?
Can your interior warmth go up a point
After so many smiles? Does each smile
Register somehow permanently in you,
Like a scar? Can you get smiling scars?
We can see the effect of smiles on faces,
The cheerful lines that smiles cut in skin
After years of use; do smiles also get cut
Into people who have been smiled upon?
If everything we know about everything
Is hardly anything, could smiles be food?

Poem in Which Ray Davies and Dave Davies Huddle at the Top of the Staircase at Their Home In Muswell Hill in London Listening to Their Aunts

And uncles and parents and older sisters guzzling and singing
Around the piano, songs from the war, songs from school days,
Songs that the uncles found in their work in factories and pubs,
Church songs, country songs, songs that people sang in shelters
As Göring's bombs spun down, and the two boys are entranced
Beyond measure. Not only with the inebriated conviviality that
Seems so alluring and will later come close to killing both boys,
But with the cross-singing, and staggered singing, and melodies
Sliding around with harmony and contrapuntal rhythm, and two
Uncles ungently banging on the piano despite the snarling piano
Player gesturing to them to bugger off and stand away, dammit!
It's an entire new language that no one in the family ever speaks
About during the day, a dangerous language, rough and thrilling
At the same time; there's sex in it somehow, and something like
The feeling you have when you scream as loud as you can. Your
Throat gets all shredded when you scream, but it also feels great,
Somehow, as if you got something out of you that couldn't come
Out any other way except that violent way. So music can be dark
And beautiful at the same time, who knew? The boys sometimes
Fall asleep there at the top of the stairs, before the music finishes,
And their dad finds them when he staggers upstairs, and he hoists
Them up onto his shoulders like sacks of wheat, or sleeping seals,
And lurches down the hallway and flops them, ungently, into bed.

Tyee

I have been writing too many condolence letters lately.
I am using the same sorts of words and the words have
Become husks of what they used to be. Like the people
I am writing about. Who are there on the page, illusory
But adamant. Good thing for ritual. How else could we
Say anything without saying anything? Could it be that
Most of what we say aims at something other than what
We say? Could that be? We use words so casually, such
Flow and fluidity and panache, but what we want to say
Are the rocks in the stream, the occasional brilliant bird,
The serpentine mink, the lugubrious heron, the drowned
Ancient fungus-riddled salmon. I am writing about tyee,
The great chinook, the king of fish, and he held adamant
Behind a boulder for a while as he began to dissolve and
Now his time has come and he slips away and I type this
To his widow using words like *my most sincere sorrows*.
She knows and I know what I mean but for a moment all
I see on the page is the weary dignity holding in the pool.

Poem for an Editor

Well, once every couple months or so I get a note from this friend
I have never met, and perhaps never will, although for many years
Now we have corresponded, and most of the notes have to do with
A bit of money due me for something I never remember, but in her
Note this friend always says, with glorious politeness, *perhaps you*
Will remember agreeing to . . ., which is hilarious, because I cannot
Remember what shirt I wore yesterday, or what essay I wrote more
Than two days ago, or whether or not I have paid that obstreperous
Medical bill that should have been paid last week, and perhaps was.
But, see, it says something about her and about me that I just adore
The word *perhaps* there. Isn't that gentle? Isn't that merciful? Sure,
It's funny—I haven't the slightest recollection of agreeing that *The*
Journal of Tall Left-Handed Samoan Albatross Studies may reprint
The piece in question, but *she* does, you see, and even as she knows
I haven't the slightest memory of it, she gently suggests that I might.
I don't know—something about this gives me great hope. It's about
Mercy and generosity somehow. There are no little things or events;
None. I am beginning to suspect that this is the theme of everything
I ever wrote or ever will write. I mean, you could write vast burbles
Of books about all this, but doesn't that sweet *perhaps* get right at it?

Near Otis, Oregon

I am no longer young and supple and pliable
And thoughtless about bending and kneeling,
So that when I am driving along one night &
See something wriggling in the road, and see
That it is a little pine squirrel, I have to think
About what to do. Think with me, brothers &
Sisters. We can do the usual, which is driving
On, knowing that nature red in tooth and claw
Will handle the cleanup; a vulture, two crows,
A delighted hungry hawk. We could also back
Up and drive over the animal, and finish it off.
We could, were we miraculously supple again,
Stop and get out and escort it off and conclude
Things, and bury it reverently, as a friend does.
I back up the car. It is a coastal road, with rare
Traffic. The rear half of the squirrel is crushed
Almost flat. Maybe a logging truck. He cannot
Have long to live. Or she. I have a golf club in
The car—am I going to beat a squirrel to death
With a putter? No. I am going to line up the car
Just right, and be sure front and back tires both
Deliver full weight, and with meditative intent,
Murder a fellow being, name unknown. Then I
Do escort it into the ferns with the putter. Only
A squirrel. But even now, long after that night,
I remember him or her, and I feel good and bad
About what I did, and wonder who she or he is,
Or was; who knows what happens to the spirits

Of living things? We imagine heavens and hell,
We talk about rebirth and how no energy is lost.
If physicists are right, as I suspect they are, who
Or what is that energy now? A crow, a bemused
Golfer, a driver of a logging truck, a salmon fry?
Or even, we might speculate, a new pine squirrel,
One totally leery of roads, for mysterious reasons.

Spectacle

I was visiting my mom and dad recently who together
Are nearly two hundred years old, and they savor naps
In the afternoon, *We believe we have earned our naps,*
As my dad says with a smile, and when they lay down
They remove their respective spectacles and fold them
Ever so carefully and place them on their night-tables,
In exactly the same places every day and night, so that
Their hands can reach out slowly gently hesitantly but
With a quiet confidence to find them when they awake.
We think that there are small things and small gestures
And insignificant daily stuff, but that is the most arrant
Nonsense. I saw the dignified hesitancy of their hands,
The calm way their hands went to meet their spectacles,
The spectacles waiting patiently. The brilliance of craft
And creativity that invented the spectacles. The sinewy
Of the hands, the lean yearn of them, the runes of scars.
I could watch their hands arise from abed, and go quest
For that which allows the shepherds of the hands to see,
I could watch that every day, watch them stir and smile
And don spectacles and say *Time for tea, do you think?*

Poem for a Guy I Knew in College
Who Was Not Actually My Friend

But I want to catch something about him anyway, because he just died,
Still young, and we always write poems about people we love and like,
But there's a subtle thing to be said about this guy, so let's tiptoe slowly
Toward it and hope we stumble across it. He was more than a bit of con
Man, to be wholly honest, and he snaked a lot of girls, and he was a sort
Of guy who smiled and said hey but he didn't really mean it, you know?
But there was some easy grace and cheer to him that wasn't always fake.
There was a decent flash in the guy that you hoped would be fanned and
Years later he would be a good guy, and when he died people would say,
And really mean it from their hearts, that he was a good guy. You could
Tell there was a good guy beneath the handsome snake—we thought so,
Anyway. So when I read his obituary and a friend said with real passion
That the deceased was *just a real good man*, that was what must be said,
I was somehow happy—not that I was right, all those years ago, but that
There was a pilot light in the guy that did get fanned into flame. The fire
Matters, and it is so easy to let it die, and it *does* die out in so many men,
Guys are born with the spark of decency, even if it is fitful, and hesitant,
And then it winked out, and they were sentenced to a long life flameless,
And they knew they had lost it, which maybe explains a murderous rage;
What a hell, to be trapped in a soul you knew full well was dark and cold.
What a prison cell, to know nobody would ever say *just a real good man*.

Here's What I Think
When I Think about That

I was in rural Nebraska the other day driving
With a man who had farmed here for seventy
Years as he said since I was almost three and
My dad had me seed a field. I was intent that
I would finish that field because I adored dad
And wanted to make him proud. I seeded just
About half and then keeled over and he came
Running and got me and give me water—and
Then he puts me on his shoulders, and we did
The rest of the field. That field's been planted
By my family for 98 years in a row. Soybeans
And corn alternately lately. Sorghum one time
That I remember and I think alfalfa occasional,
I'd have to go look through the books to check.
Sure, I've thought about selling it. I don't have
Kids and the niece I might give it to isn't much
For farming. Might sell it in a year or two, sure.
But here's what I think when I think about that:
What would the field think when someone else
Plowed and seeded and weeded and harvested?
You know what I mean? Sounds crazy, but I've
Thought about it, sure. You get to know a field
Pretty well. Its moods and habits. It allows deer
But it does not like raccoons so much, I believe.
That sort of thing. I know this sounds nutty, but

Then again I know every inch of that field. And
Two feet deep of it too. Maybe it knows me too.
It could be. Well, here you are. Pleasure to chat.

Their Raptorish Privacy

Spent a week with a sharp-shinned hawk recently,
In a manner of speaking; I lived briefly where she
Or he appears to live all the time, or just this year;
I couldn't tell how ancient the nest, or if there was
Still a mortgage on it. I looked for teenage graffiti,
Or for sneakers piled on the edge like at our house,
But I didn't see any of that. I did see a wonderfully
Disguised nest, though. It was in a tangle of spruce
And it was so artfully placed that it took long hours
For me to finally nail arriving and departing flights
To source and destination. I just wanted to see how
And where the nest was. My dangerous knowledge,
I realized, after I acquired it; I now knew his refuge,
Or hers, maybe theirs; their home, their tiny shelter,
Built of wood and down and the skeletons of rabbit;
Perhaps their nest was what mine is to me, a silence
Occasionally filled with the small noises that a lover
And your shared progeny make; the small squabbles,
The subtle surrenders, the shared meals; your huddle
Against the tempestuous world. I had drawn the nest,
Even sketched a rough map, thinking idly to share it
With my sons who are also agape at hawkish beings;
But I put it in the fire, from some sort of urge toward
Respect for the neighbors and their raptorish privacy.

The Tree Surgeon Talks about Good Wood

Friend of mine took down an old red cedar over the last two days.
We talked about the tree for a while today, as he prepared to grub
The stump, as he said. Poor old thing, he said. All rotted out from
Top to bottom. He wasn't quite dead but he was sure nearly there.
It is a mercy to take him down. We can only imagine what he felt
Like without his interior parts. Crumbling away quietly. Poor guy.
See there where the trunk went to three trunks? I might have built
A table from that was he not so punk inside. No, there's no decent
Wood left to work. He's firewood. Just kindling. Cedar burns real
Fast. How old is he? Eighty maybe. Maybe a hundred. Saw a great
Deal, he did. The Columbus Day storm, ice storms, snow. All sorts
Of birds and insects lived in and around him, I guess. See the hole
There, that probably started with insects and then went to birds and
Finally maybe flying squirrels or such. Poor old thing. It's good for
Him to come down, for all sorts of reasons, but one is, well, respect.
He's a lot older than we are and wiser in ways than we do not know.
That's a fact. I am not much for getting all wavygravy about a cedar
Coming down, and he'll be kindling for probably most of the winter,
But you have to acknowledge a life when you take it, it seems to me,
So let this be his funeral, you and me looking at his old weary bones.
You want some of the wood? I'll make up a box and leave it for you.
In fact if there's enough good wood I'll make the box out of him too.

The Hurling Match

One time years ago I was driving along the shore of Galway Bay
With my lovely bride and our burbling children when we noticed
A game in full roar in the distance a bit. We were in no hurry and
For once we didn't even have a destination so we wandered along
What was not even a dirt road until we found the game. It was to
My absolute delight a hurling match—Bearna against An Spidéal,
Neighboring towns along the wine-dark sea. We stood there awed
At the speed and skill of the players. They were just kids but good
Lord Almighty they were deft and slippery with their hurley sticks
And the ball smaller than a baseball. We gawped and tried silently
To figure out the geometry of the game, its flow and laws, its song,
In a manner of speaking; games have a lyricism of their own, none
Quite like the others, though they may be cousins, and one genuine
Pleasure in seeing a game for the first time is trying to make out its
Music. One of us remarked the constant collisions, *the precipitance
Of violence*, as she said; others were nailed by the whirring hurleys,
Flashing like axes or staves or cudgels in the fat sunlight; and me, I
Was entranced by how the players somehow had eight senses going
At once, and were able to evade crashes and scything and smashing,
All of which seemed so immediately imminent; another of the great
Things about sports is how the players magically do *not* get crushed
And hammered and flattened and mangled; we never talk about this,
But for all the attention to scoring and victories and ferocious effort,
It's the way players survive without damage, evade with grace, slide
Out of trouble with a half-smile that amazes and moves me the most.
I haven't the slightest idea who won the game. I think it was Bearna,
As they had a glorious team that year, a man in the pub told me later.

Three thousand years we have been playing *Iománaíocht* in this land,
He said, and looks like Bearna will finally win a flag. A meaner man,
Now, would note that it's only the junior team, but *I* am not that man.

Miraculum

Thesis: What we commonly think of as Miracles, are mere
Synchronicities, felicitous accidents, startling coincidences;
Whereas that which we call common *is* actually miraculous.
Whoa; let's approach this slowly from the side, as we would
Edge up shy and careful to a sleeping wolverine. Wolverines
Are good to start with, come to think of it—I mean, consider
A wolverine carefully. A whopping big one weighs less than
Half the dogs you know, not to mention those two obese cats,
Yet bears and cougars and even the most stupendously stupid
Men back away from wolverines. They have been revered by
People who know them well for years beyond counting. They
Own their place. They were designed by immeasurable years.
There are only a few of them, compared to, for example, ants.
Are they not miraculous? Do they not inspire a reverent awe?
Can any of us make any of those? No? Can it be that miracles
Are things which we cannot comprehend or construct? Hawks,
Elk, porpoises, children, damselflies, quasars—the list cannot
Ever end, because every time we discover something, we also
Discover more that we don't know yet, isn't that certainly so?
So that which is miraculous is quotidian. While the occasional
Inexplicable recovery, the avoidance of death and mayhem by
The thinnest of margins, that only happens on occasion, right?
So because it isn't quotidian, perhaps it isn't a miracle. Listen,
I know your brain is buzzling right about now—it's happening
To me too. But the thought that miracles are normal, isn't that
The cool thought of the day? Let's remember that until dinner,
You and me, and then savor the miracles with whom we dine.

Just Now Right Now

Or here's a story. A man and a woman have two kids
Together, a girl and a boy, three years apart, and then
The mother walks out the door one day when the kids
Are five and two and never ever comes back. The dad
Does his best to raise the kids, and he does a good job,
Says the daughter who is now thirty, but then she tells
Me one little detail that gives me the shivering willies.
Every year on her brother's birthday she forged a card
From the mother to the son. Every year. Sixteen years.
That sixteenth year when he opened the card he stared
Up at his sister. This kind of thing happens every other
Minute in every country on earth. All you can do is say
Nothing with your heart open for all the little kids who
Are staring at their sisters just now right now just then.

How to Dress for Your Wedding

Arise ye early in the morning and begin to go through
The usual peregrinations of your morning ritual before
Realizing with a stagger that this is o my God the Day.
Sit right down there in the kitchen and hold your brain
In both hands so your head does not fly into a hundred
Bits which would be bad because we do not have time
To clean even though a dirty kitchen is a mortification
To the soul and rightly so. This is something to discuss
With the woman who will be Your Spouse along about
One o'clock this afternoon, if all goes well. Certainly it
Will *not* go smoothly because *you* are involved and An
Epic Shamble of Disasters, as a brother has called your
Previous romantic entanglements, haunts you just now,
At the kitchen table, because they never lasted, or were
Deep and rich and true, mostly because you were a dolt,
Although you have also thought quietly in the nether of
The night that the problem always was you did not love
Them, and were not yet honest enough to say so bluntly.
But this woman you *do* love, thoroughly; this woman is
The only one you can imagine leaping off the edge with;
And whether this will end well, whether this will endure
And grow deeper and more mysterious and complicated
As you go along, whether you will find ways to disagree
Agreeably and productively and nutritiously, and remain
Your own best selves while elevating the other somehow,
Whether you will have the humor and bruises of children
Inflicted upon you by the Chief Musician; this is not your
Primary concern right now. Right now you need two cups

Of coffee, and a shower, and then the suit, and the shining
Shoes, and that damned bow tie, whose idea was it to have
An actual bow tie that you have to actually tie? But we tie
It, eventually, trying not to curse, and then, shivering a bit,
Even though it's a brilliant day, we drive slowly to church.

What We Think We Forget

Sometimes, even now, in my sixth decade on this earth,
Even though I am graced beyond all other men because
I am allowed to sleep alongside the alluring conundrum
Of my remarkable wife, I still, in the last seconds before
I get to sleep, occasionally remember sleeping alongside
My brother, even though that was fifty years ago, and far
Away, and we are now hirsute & opinionated older gents.
Still, though, once in a while I am eight, and he is asleep,
And he is seven, and it is Saturday, and we can sleep late,
Or, even better, get up early to watch cartoons, in silence,
Because if no one wakes up then no one can tell us not to,
And we are in our pajamas, eating cereal silently, asprawl
On the cushions, and it is always sunny even when it isn't.
How is it that what we experienced we always experience,
And even what we think we forget is never actually gone?
How could that be? You can misplace it, or misfile it, and
There are a thousand ways that it can be hidden or shoved
Behind another memory, like boxes huddled in dark attics,
But it turns out it's always there whether you want it to be
Or not, and occasionally there it is again, incontrovertible,
And I am eight, and he is seven, and there is cereal, and it
Is sunny, even when it isn't. Even when it rained it didn't.

The Western Yellowjacket: A Note

September, and the yellowjackets are desperate; these are the males,
Soon to die, but committed, before they go, to hauling in every kind
Of meat they can find, for the next generation, hidden in secret loam;
So the fading rangers scour every chance, every picnic and barbecue,
Every patch of grass, and when they find a shred of sausage, a fallen
Burger, a scrap of fat, they dicker and deconstruct it with astonishing
Speed and celerity. I could watch them all afternoon. They are fading
Even as they labor with such assiduity; they must know that they will
Outlast their own largesse by only a few weeks, if that; yet they never
Stop scouting sandwiches, and pouncing on popsicles, and quartering
The school picnic. Isn't it the case that everything is a teacher finally?
Everything speaks clearly if you can decipher the language, the music.
Everything. And in the end what you learn best is that you don't know
Anything well; everything never stops singing. Isn't that what we both
Have learned over the course of our lives? That there is a sort of music
That we can hear but never explain, except by talking sort of sideways,
About wasps, for example, or gods, or mathematics, or huddled larvae.

The Peach Pie

My grandmother made the most wonderful pies.
She very occasionally made the most wonderful
Bread, loaves that drew butter to them like Jesus
Drew disciples and disgruntled religious powers.
But what I recall today is not the alluring smells,
The perfect crinks in the crust, the extraordinary
Savory unbelievably delicious tastes, the way we
Would all be silent and reverent at such glorious
Flavor, the way someone would always whimper
Happily and quietly, the way the pie would taste
Even better tomorrow—if it even lasted that long.
No—what I remember is that when I asked to cut
The first piece, she would say No!, curtly, firmly.
Nor could my next brother cut it. Our sister could,
And our mom and dad, and our older brother, and
Any aunt or uncle, and of course the parish priest.
But not us. Never. We stopped asking, eventually.
You would think a child would not remember this
But I still feel the lash of the way she said no—*of*
Course you cannot, was the message. *Who do you*
Think you are to ask such a thing? For the longest
Time when I was a boy I felt bad for me, at things
Like this; but perhaps one of the moments I began
To grow up was when I felt worse for the boy my
Brother used to be. You'd think a child would not
Remember such a slight thing, but I jot this proem
To remind you that this is, of course, not so. A kid
Remembers everything, and whatever you say to a

Kid, and especially the way you say it, is engraved
In that kid somehow somewhere, and occasionally
It bleeds, for no reason, like statues suddenly weep.

The Things We Say When We Have Nothing to Say

If I was to ask you a question about where you came from,
And you were to ask me did I mean nativity or ethnicity or
Nationality or religious background, and I said no, I meant
What story, what amazement, what joy, what ocean, would
You be speechless? I don't think so. I think you would wait
A moment to clear away all the orthodox answers, and then
You would say something like I am from people who dance
When they are sad, or I come from music I cannot run from,
Or I came through a broken door and it took me a long time
To stop trying to shatter it or repair it or inflict it on my kids.
You would say something like that, I think, if I asked gently
And we had the time to let all the other answers trundle past
Like the things we say when we actually have nothing to say.

Poem in Which Four Men, after Hauling Flowers from a Church After a Funeral, Discuss Poetics

So much depends upon the red wheelbarrow,
As the poet says, but I am here to report that
He wasn't kidding, and everything really *did*
Depend on the red kid's wagon a guest found
In the church bathroom right after the funeral.
Good thing, too, because it would have taken
A week to get all those flowers out otherwise.
This took a while. No one said much. At long
Last we were done and two guys lit cigarettes.
No one said anything for a while and then one
Guy said Remember that wheelbarrow poem?
William Carlos Williams? And we all laughed
Because we did all remember being mystified
As to why exactly it's so anthologized; it's the
Very definition of gnomic, as the janitor noted.
Now *this* red wagon, continued the wry janitor,
So much depended on it for real; the quotidian
Is poetic, the guy was right, but it's also useful
When you have to haul tons of flowers. I'd say
Useful is more poetic than poetic. But William
Carlos Williams knew that, right? He's the guy
Who wrote *no ideas but in things*. Plus the man
Was a *doctor*. Doctors know useful all too well.

The Most Arrogant Knife

What authors have influenced you most over the years?
Is the question from a girl in the back of the classroom,
And for once the usual answers do not bubble out swift
And shapely, R. L. Stevenson and Elwyn Brooks White,
And Orwell and Twain and Steinbeck and Cather and Li
Po and Henry Lawson; no, this time out comes a parade
Of stories in all sorts of shapes that nailed me somehow
In permanent and unforgettable ways: bluefish and jazz,
Basketballs and layers of fog against hills of Douglas fir,
Marten and brothers and incense and the first time I read
Whitman. Doesn't everyone remember how amazements
Knocked on their innermost doors? I saw a kestrel swoop
Out of a scrawny tree, falling like the most arrogant knife,
When I was about twelve years old; I can see it even now,
A shimmering fist in a vacant lot underneath the railroad
Tracks, a nondescript moment that was anything but that;
That's an author that affected me greatly, I'd say; and did.

Poem for a Quiet Lady at Saint Patrick's Church in Oregon

Spent two hours this morning in a wooden church away out in farm
Country—hop vines, and vineyards, and corn, and hazelnut thickets
Like tall gnarled orderly parades of broad green bedraggled soldiers.
There were seventy ladies in the church knitting prayer shawls. You
Wouldn't believe how many prayer shawls seventy ladies can create
In five hours. They told me they had made thousands of them, every
Color you could imagine, every size, untold combination of patterns.
They donated them to hospices; they gave them to neighbors in pain.
Their reward for their labor was sandwiches and cinnamon rolls way
Bigger than a baby's head. One lady in the corner was knitting small
Blankets of some shimmering shade I couldn't quite name. I asked if
They were prayer shawls and she said Oh, no, these are for stillborns.
I make these so that the parents will have something intimate instead
Of hospital issue. Every one of these is for a child who came so close
To this world. I finish one and then sit for a moment and think of that
Child, that one child who will wear this blanket, if only for a moment.
She finished speaking and she and I looked at each other for a minute,
And then I touched her shoulder to try to say something I couldn't say
With any words I know yet, and then I drove home, amazed yet again
At the huge immense glorious things being done every moment every
Where and you will never hear about a millionth of them, except once
In a while, by chance, by accident, as you glance at a corner of a page.

Poem for a Friend to Whom I Wrote Every Week

But who died last night, deep into her nineties, and my first thought,
After that bleak sagging suddenly-emptied feeling that we all know,
Is what about your address? Where am I going to send my drawings
And notes and silly poems? I have your address burnt into my brain,
I scribble it every week, and you open my note at your kitchen table,
And grin, and once a month you jot a card in that spidery meticulous
Script with which you took notes as a young Girl Reporter long ago,
And I sit here, having just read the news, feeling bad for your lonely
Kitchen table. The teacups, the mug with eighteen pens, the notepad
By your telephone. Probably there is a mountain of mail on the table.
Probably most of the mail is bills. But there are four or five missives
From people who admired you, who savored your elegant endurance,
Who laughed aloud when you piloted that glorious ancient *motorcar,*
As you called it, down the hill to town, so carefully, so painstakingly.
That's one word I might have played with in a note to you today, Lee:
Painstaking. You took pains to be amused and generous and gracious.
Ah, now, *gracious*—that's the better and best word for how you lived.
That's the word I will place on the kitchen table for you this morning.

Swagger

My son reminds me of a moment when he was two years old.
He was about two feet tall then. Now he is about six feet tall;
He has tripled, as he says. But then he was in his stroller, and
His mother was trundling him down the hospital hallway, and
He had just come through a second heart surgery with roaring
Colors, as his doctor said, and we were thrilled and exhausted
And worn and rattled and happier than I could ever find words
For then or now, and as we got toward the exits our son sat up
And said *walk*. Now, here's a child who just got cut open stem
To stern, and got his interior parts re-plumbed, and there's silk
& copper and platinum and Gore-Tex inside him meticulously
Stitched together to create a system whereby he doesn't expire,
And he's only two and fully capable of falling down head over
Heels or suddenly running off and crashing into a weary nurse,
But he was pretty firm about what he wanted, and we were not
In a position to argue, being totally wiped out emotionally and
Every other way, so my wife gently unbuckles him and he gets
Out and swaggers out through the doors himself. He didn't tip-
Toe or stroll or walk or shuffle or amble or shamble or waddle.
I choose the word carefully: swagger. He was all major attitude.
It was, really and truly, like he was making a statement with his
Body, with the eloquent way he walked. We stood there gaping.
I remember the slight rustle of his infinitesimal leather slippers.
The little moments that are not little. The huge revolving doors.
And then my bride sweeping him up, and walking and weeping.

The Best Rebounder I Ever Had

The best rebounder I ever had was a burly friend who didn't see well,
But he could see well enough that he could perceive the bright orange
Basketball caroming off the rim, and he would set himself to obtain it,
Which he did quite often because he was mammoth and committed to
His task with a rare and admirable devotion, and after he snared a ball
He would look for me, and believe me I was present within his limited
Eyesight range, because even I, not the brightest of bulbs, realized that
Each rebound he hauled out of the pack was another possession for me,
So if Big Chris was banging away for fifteen rebounds a game, I would
Have fifteen more handles, which would mean another ten shots, given
That I would have to give it up at least five times for appearance's sake.
I actually thought this way. And an extra ten shots would mean perhaps
Four buckets, which would be eight points, plus the foul here and there.
I actually thought this way. So I figured my friend Big Chris was easily
Worth nine points a game, plus he defended like a nut, plus he dropped
Eight or ten points on his own from heroic hard labor in the seething pit
In the lane where no sensible guard needed to go, especially as Chrisser
Was hauling down rebounds for me. I loved calculating what guys were
Worth: our cheerful useless center was worth minus nine points a game,
As he would happily give up more points than he earned; our invaluable
Point guards were worth ten plus points a game easily, as they were fast
Sneaky effective two-turnover guys who played great defense and loved
To pass and drove whenever they wanted to and could even shoot, when
They were in the mood. But it says something about me then, and I type
This now with a rueful smile, that I never calculated my own true worth;
I counted only by points, and never subtracted hilarious defensive faults,
And an amazing reluctance to pass the ball, and fitful rebounding labors,
And a total reluctance to take off on the break after a rebound, because I

Would be standing next to Chris, who would, to his credit always gently
Hand me the ball. Sometimes I would even touch him on the elbow if he
Hadn't seen me lurking for the ball, and he would turn and hand it to me,
Ever so carefully. You know, I started this poem as a confessional, about
How finally goofily selfish I was as a player and how entertaining that is,
At least now, to look back on, but let's end it with a small lovely gesture,
A teammate's gesture, with something like humor and camaraderie in it —
Big Chris ever so carefully handing me the ball he had just plucked from
The air filled with elbows and curses and grunts and thuds; and off we go.

Questions I Was Asked
Today by Sixth-Graders

How did you really become you?
Do you dream in whole paragraphs?
Are you still a writer if you stop writing?
Do you have to be a citizen to publish here?
What was the first sentence you ever wrote?
Do you have to be 21 to publish as a writer?
Is a good story still good in other languages?
Is writing better if you type it or scribble it first?
Do ideas come to you or do you go looking for them?
Do you have to wear black if you want to be a writer?
Do movies have writers on the set to fix story problems?
Are your children embarrassed when you write about them?
Did you know your essay seems to have several meanings at once?
Are your parents happy you are a writer or were they hoping for money?
If we want to ask you more questions, do we have to write them or can we text?

Yes

I was on a gleaming elevator in a vast hotel in a huge city
The other day when a man got on with his daughter about
Age four. I asked her what floor they wanted and she said
Seven million. I reached up as high as I could and pressed
An imaginary button and she laughed and some little door
Opened in all three of us, a wordless yes, and we started to
Talk about the elevator's voice, which sounded like a lady
From Ireland or Scotland, and how the buttons were twice
As big as any giant's fingers, and how older gents like me
Remembered buildings without thirteenth floors, isn't that
Funny, that an ancient superstition would still be reflected
In modern buildings? By now the girl was dancing and her
Dad and I were grinning at her ebullience but then the lady
Spoke their floor and the door opened. The girl leapt away,
But the dad hesitated a second and said quietly *hey thanks*,
And I knew just what he meant—something like thanks for
Being four years old for a minute. We have those moments
When we are all the same age, from the same country, with
The same language on our teeth, and it never lasts too long,
But it always feels weirdly familiar, doesn't it? Like we are
Home again for a moment, with family we hardly get to see.

Finally Is a Lot Further Away
Than Sick Ever Expected

A friend of mine is unhealably ill but somehow this does not
Define and explain and crouch foremost in his life and labors.
This nails me. How can this be? When *I* am sick, there's Sick
And then there's everything else. Not him, though—he'll talk
About it guardedly if you ask but it's like he made a deal with
Sick to be mere companions, and he refuses to give sick pride
Of place. I wonder if his sick gets peeved about this. Gets sort
Of pissy, you know, and sticks a needle in just to get attention.
I wouldn't be startled if my friend and his sick have had a few
Blunt conversations about who's in charge of the boat for now.
My friend is not the kind of man to get into a pissing war with;
He's got a falcon stare that gives you the willies, and his grasp
Of fact when he puts his mind to it is oceanic. So he knows all
About his sick, and how to keep it at arm's length, and force it
To sleep outside in the shed, whereas his sick doesn't yet fully
Understand my friend. It's like they are locked in a grim chess
Game that sick will win finally but finally is a lot further away
Than sick ever expected and sick is none too happy about this.
There are a lot of days when I am pittering along and suddenly
Think of my friend, and while often then I wince, because he's
A wry generous man and he added lots of light to the universe,
Just as often I grin, thinking of his disgruntled sick. Screw you,
I would say to his sick, if we were sitting across the chess table
From each other. You took on a prickly obdurate character and
Now you are stuck with him and you can't escape either. Me, I
Hope you get so sick and tired of not being the star of his show

84

That you quit, but even if that is not possible, I hope you detest
Every day that he refuses to let you tell him who and how to be.
That's what I hope—that you hate every day the rest of his life.

Poem in Which Dave Kingman Hits a Home Run That Is Amazingly Still Traveling 36 Years Later

Because why not? No one ever actually *saw* it land, although
People tell stories of it running north along Kenmore Avenue
Maybe all the way to Wisconsin, or even Canada. It could be
That the ball skidded right over Baffin Bay and concluded its
Career in Nunavut. Who is to say? I heard it leave his bat; I'd
Opened my window, five blocks away, and I knew he was up,
Because Lou Boudreau had just murmured it, and there was a
Flat sharp rude inarguable snapping sound—not quite a crack,
As the usual phraseology has it—and an instant later I heard a
Swell of voices that sounded eerily like serious surf. Kingman
Was having a terrific season that year, at last hitting for points
As well as power, and he hit lots of other homers, but that one
Rivets me, because if I still remember it, then it is still just hit,
Somehow, isn't it? It's still the exact instant when the ball has
Been reversed, and has left his bat, at a hundred miles an hour,
And is headed directly north, over the left field wall, or maybe
Into another poem altogether: If no one saw it land, then could
It arrive hilariously in someone else's poem? Couldn't that be?
Imagine wonderful shy wry wise Mary Oliver's astonishment!
I suppose it is a quantum ball, being hit and not yet hit and not
Yet landed all at the same time; and I am sure it has not landed
Quite yet because, well, here we are, hearing it, from a number
Of blocks and years later—a sharp snap, and then crashing surf.

Skiffling Shuffling Skittering Scuffling

As I am sitting at the stoplight under the maple and oak and cedar trees
I see three tiny kids skiffling and shuffling and skittering and scuffling
In the leaves—bigleaf maples, mostly, but also some oak, and a serious
Drift of fir and cedar needles—*duff* is the word for that, a delicious one,
Is it not? They are maybe five years old, these three moppets, and I hear
Their bus groaning a ways behind me, but they are totally into sculpting
Little hills and ridges of leaves, and I can hear them giggling, and in one
Minute the bus will hold out its arms and absorb them, and the parade is
Starting to move in front of me, but for another perfect instant I can hear
And see them skiffling and giggling, and smell the sharp savory death of
The brilliant leaves, and see the shoulder of the mom or aunt or neighbor
In the lee of the apartment building, where she is just lighting a cigarette,
And we get these moments all day long, don't we, we get them all month
And week and year all our lives, such a flood and flow of them, too many
To count, too many to endure, they are too generous and savory and holy,
We could not bear to see and savor and sing them all; we would go blind.
But without them we would starve and wither and shrink and shrivel. We
Know that too. Maybe custom and habit and the quotidian ramble are just
The things we need to keep us from being overwhelmed by the profligacy
Of miracle, the huge of the tiny, the gift of every single thing there ever is.
But we also peek and glance and notice the light through the bars we built.
I bet you are like me and you crave the unbearable light but bless the bars;
And if ever we needed a wry working definition of *human being*, that's it.

Best Day *Ever*

Met a small girl this morning carrying a very large stuffed dog
Very nearly her size, and when I asked her what she called her
Dog she said today his name is Trousers. Tomorrow he will be
Very Nearly, I think. We decide his name in the morning when
We wake up; usually he tells me but sometimes I hear it before
He does and I get to tell him. It's a game between us. His other
Names this week were Mac and Cheese, that was this weekend,
And this was so funny that we laughed all day long, on Sunday.
Did you ever laugh one whole day? Isn't that the best day *ever*?

The First Layer of Favorite

Sir, asks the high school student this morning,
What are your favorite subjects to read about?
And I answer, suddenly, in a great happy burst,
Angels, butter, otters, letters, surfing, airplanes,
Guitars, basketball, bruised grace, children, elk,
Tuna, paleontology, scissors, newspapers, dales,
Rills, Wales, seas, hawks, anything about ships,
Defiant courage, adamant tenderness, maniacal
Insistence on patience, the wonder of endurance,
Pillows, tides, languages, music, all sorts of hats,
Epiphanic moments, cities, forests of every kind,
Everything having to do with the effects of time,
Connemara, zygotes, the birds of Hawaii, cheese
In every possible form, the sport of cricket, kites
(the bird, such as the swallow-tailed, not the toy),
Bears, anthropology, religions, wolverines, foxes,
Obituaries, cosmology, and anything about wines.
Report cards, letters sent by my dad to my mother
During the Second World War when they thought
He would die for sure, so his letters are somehow
Loaded with love and fraught with fearful dignity.
Anything about the woman who married me, who
Remains a complete and utter mystery, even after
We have lived together for thirty years. Does that
Answer your question sufficiently, or do we need
To poke into the next layer of favorite? We good?

Holy and Fearsome

In a chapel the other morning I asked a lot of people
To write down the worst six words they'd ever heard
In their lifetimes, but don't tell me or say them aloud,
I said, I just want you to dive down into your bruised
Places and touch the words, sort of to prove we don't
Forget anything, but also to remember how a handful
Of words can be daggers and viruses carrying despair,
Words are huge and powerful and holy and fearsome,
And everyone stares at their laps, and people scribble,
And for once I shut my mouth and leave the haunting
Moment alone, but then one guy in the front row says
Very quietly, You want to hear mine? Mine are these:
Dad, you love me too much. He said it so quietly that
I am fairly sure I was the only one who heard what he
Said, and after a second or two the morning hurried on,
But I keep thinking about those words, and about how
He looked at me as he whispered them, and I couldn't
Tell if my question had been a strange gift, or a punch.

Owls Are the Bears of the Sky

Owls are the bears of the sky, a small boy informs me the other day.
I think they are cousins. They don't say much, and they have really
Thick coats, and no one picks on them, and they like to live around
Trees, and they don't care if it's cold, and they have claws. It could
Be that they have dinner together sometimes. *You never know*, says
My mom. *You just never know.* She says that all the time about lots
Of things but especially animals. We talk about animals all the time.
She gets tired of reading about them, but *I* never ever get tired, there
Are so *many* animals, and so many *kinds* of animals, and there's not
One person in the world who knows everything about animals, even
God does not know everything about animals, because God said Let
There be animals, and then even *God* was startled at what happened!
That's what my mom says, and when I ask her about more stories of
How that happened she says *you never know*, but we can *try* to know,
So that's what I am going to do, find out about all the animals. What
Could be a cooler life than that? Starting with the bears and the owls.

Whatever It Is You Think You Are Chasing, You Just Ran Away from It

A friend tells me this story the other day: His one daughter
Was about to give birth when her husband abandoned ship,
Absconding for parts unknown with a different companion
Than the one he had sworn to honor and respect all his life.
He left a note on the kitchen table. She went into labor four
Hours later. This is a true story, says my friend, and we ran
To the house and got her to the hospital, and on the way we
All somehow agreed not to mention the husband ever again,
But we did so without a word being spoken. Isn't that wild?
And a little later I was the first man ever to cradle this child.
I was the first man who ever cradled our own calm daughter.
I feel so lucky. I'll never speak that man's name again, but I
Could say this: whatever it is you think you are chasing, you
Just ran away from it—that's what I would say to *that* slime.

A Shy Expedition

Anyone who wears spectacles while awake will know
This particular subtle private silent quotidian moment:
The way you assign one of your hands, ever so gently,
To go find your spectacles on the night-table—ideally
Where they were when you removed them and folded
Them carefully and even perhaps reverently, like I do,
For I never lose the boyish delight at being able to *see*
Because bright folks invented my spidery implements.
Your hand does not thrash or flail, or lumber or grope;
It does not trundle or clank or bang: It's more of a shy
Expedition, like a first date, with much the same eager
Pleasure and trepidation, the same possibility for crash
Or caress, in that instant when the hand is up and away
From headquarters, and hoping to, ever so gently, land.

Could There Be a Badger Jesus?

You want to hear a resurrection story? I'll tell you
A resurrection story. I saw a squirrel get squished
In the street. This was on Ash Street, near where a
Family named Penance lives. Things like this rivet
Me. Religions don't live in churches. Religions are
Not about religion, in the end; they're vocabularies.
This squirrel got *hammered*. I mean, a car ran right
Over it, and the car sped down the hill, and I recall
Thinking that some dog would soon be delighted to
Be rolling ecstatically in squirrel oil, but then, even
As I watched, the animal resumed its original shape
And staggered off into the laurel thicket, inarguably
Alive and mobile, if somewhat rattled and unkempt.
Jesus and Lazarus must have known that feeling, of
Being sore in every joint, and utterly totally fixated
On a shower and coffee and a sandwich. Or walnuts,
Depending, I suppose, on species. Our current form
Is a nebulous idea, is what I am trying to say. Could
It be that resurrections are normal and the one we're
Always going on about in the Christian mythologies
Is only One a long time ago, when there are millions
Per day? Could there be an insect Jesus and a badger
Jesus and a salmon Jesus? Could there be impossible
Zillions of Jesuses? Isn't that really the whole point?

The Antipodean Comma

A high school student asks me innocently about
The rules for commas, and my mouth opens and
Out falls all sorts of cheerful nonsense, like why,
There's the anticipatory, comma, the one, that is
Like learning how to use a gear shift, and there's
The capital Comma, which is always spelled out,
And there are the northern commas, used only at
The head of a page, and the Antipodean Comma,
Which is always printed upside down. The whole
Class is staring at me now, and the teacher gapes,
And then I fall into an interminable discussion of
The Oxford or serial comma which I love and use
All the time because Billy Blake did and he was a
Genius and no mistake. The bell rings finally and
A boy comes up to me and says, I think you were
Just riffing for fun there, sir, but I have to say that
Was the first time I *ever* thought that punctuation
Isn't the most boring thing ever invented. Maybe.

And Then There Is This

Here is who is really cool. Here is who is really
Admirable and to be emulated and what is holy:
The few people who get up instantly when their
Sister is suddenly sick, in awful ways, at dinner.
They just jumped up and dealt with it. It's dirty,
And there's no advantage in it, no money or sex,
No fame, nothing but stench and bleah and eww,
And then a young woman sat with the sick sister,
Letting her rattled sick aunt lean on her shoulder.
I saw all this. There's all this talk, and then there
Is this. You know exactly what I am saying here.

Cards That Are Good for Scraping Ice off Your Car

For some reason it seems to me that debit cards are better for this morning task:
This might mean something subtle and interesting about financial responsibility.
Grocery store cards also seem denser and stronger than any other sorts of cards;
What could that possibly mean? That foodstuffs, being basic to life, are primary
In other areas of life? Library cards, I notice, are also excellent, which somehow
Is a deep relief to me, that the badge of literacy and curiosity doesn't snap under
Pressure, but easily and smoothly removes obstacles to progress and exploration.
I can hear you thinking that I am a nut, and who thinks about what kinds of cards
Are best for scraping ice off your mirrors and windows?, and why not just invest
In an ice scraper? But then we would not have had this private moment to ponder
The whole matter of credit v. debit cards, and how insurance cards are poor stuff,
And isn't it the case that every little thing like this is fascinating, especially when
You consider that we only get the one life, as far as we can tell, and in this lovely
One life every single thing and moment and detail is a thread of the most thrilling
Fabric ever? Isn't that so? It turns out there are no tiny things, not at all, not at all.
You know what I mean: an owl feather, the broken fingernail of a small child, the
Way the child gazes raptly at the feather and trusts me utterly while I trim the nail.

Poem in Which a Love Letter Floats over Western South Dakota

One time I was driving with a friend of mine through the Great American Desert,
Which is what a huge section of the middle of America used to be called because
It was killingly hot or cold, and two trees were an occasion for huge celebrations,
And you could go for an amazingly long way before you hit water wider than you,
And we had been driving for such a long while that we had achieved not speaking
Except occasionally, which, when you think about it, is a mark of deep friendship,
Because all the small talk has been boiled away, and you chat only when you have
Something to actually say, which is unnerving at first but then refreshing; and as it
Was getting shocking hot, my friend rolled down his window, and the letter he had
Been writing to his girl, a letter that had stretched on to maybe ten pages, fluttered
Out of the window and away into the desert. Yes, I stopped the car, after I stopped
Laughing so hard I sprained an eyeball, and yes, he roared off to reclaim his words,
But what I remember this morning is the way the letter flew out of the car instantly,
Delightedly, inarguably; do you know what I mean? It was like it had been waiting
For just this chance, and it whipped out of the window and away across the grasses
And asters and antelopes and foxes and ferrets and owls and voles and prairie dogs.
I disremember now if he found all the pages, or if a few pages had been anointed in
Their travels, edited by the desert, stamped by the residents, but I do remember that
We laughed ourselves silly, and that much later, in a library in Kansas, I spread out
Every book I could find about the Great American Desert to see what sort of beings
His love letter had floated over or under; and even now, all these years later, I think
Sometimes about a mouse reading a page, and a burrowing owl snagging two pages
And reading them with raised eyebrows, and a falcon flipping over in the air to read
Bits of pages four and seven, before the wind catches it, and then, finally, the author.

Nailed by Wonder

One time when my brother and I were young we were on the beach
As usual as always as often as we could possibly be, and we pawed
Through the wrack line for odd shells and net-floats and fish-bones
And occasional wonders like wood stamped with another language;
And this afternoon we found dozens of small black things with four
Horns, as it were, two at each end, like tiny pallets. These were egg-
Cases for sharks and rays, a lifeguard explained; they washed up on
The shore every year at about this time, after the tiny fish inside had
Wriggled out. The cases were created of collagen, said the lifeguard,
Which is a substance we have in our bodies also, boys. Probably this
Is a skate's case, although there are sharks here who lay eggs and we
Find the cases on the beach. See, now, here's the hole where the tiny
Fish got out. I'd better get back to work now, boys, and he went back
Up on his stand and we wandered away but I remember that we were
Both nailed by wonder, and contemplating the great silent mothers in
The sea, sliding along behind the surf, leaving their children in tough
Black envelopes among the rocks and tangles. We were both *startled*,
Is what I want to poke at. We didn't know and then we knew, and we
Were thrilled and a little frightened. Isn't that the right state of mind?
Isn't that how we live most of this life, rattled by how much we don't
Know, and don't know even what we are absolutely certain we know,
And then again and again floored by the tiny things that are not at all?

The Slight Light

Had a pint with a friend last night and afterward we lingered
On the street corner for a while talking about this and that &
The other thing. That's all—nothing pressing or momentous.
But the thought occurs to me that the itch to linger was itself
Momentous, all the more so because both of us were pleased
To casually extend the conversation. Just that, nothing heavy
Here, no moral, no piercing illumination. Just the slight light
Of a small good thing, a quiet pleasure, a tiny thing that isn't.
So much of what makes your life a pleasure is this very thing
That we fumble to articulate: Your son setting the table, your
Mom's lovely adamant handwriting, the librarian very gently
Slipping a receipt into your mound of films because he gets it
That you will only remember to remember when they are due
When you get home. So many miniscule mountainous things.

A Swirl of Affectionate Air

Here is what I miss this morning: jamming my forearm into the small
Of my older taller wider brother's back, and shoving this forearm into
Him with all my might, so much so that I would have been very proud
To have moved him a quarter of an inch, which did not happen, and he
Chuckled quietly that I was working so hard to hold my territory, as he
Inched inevitably infinitesimally massively closer to the basket, and all
This as I was swiping at the ball with my other hand and unaccidentally
Cracking him on the hand and arm. It took him about four long minutes
To get from the foul line down close enough to the basket where he, not
A fine shooter, could score; and while usually right about here the poem
Would mention whether or not he scored, that's not what we are here for.
This is about me all delighted at shoving him as hard as I possibly could
And him being honored that I was shoving him, and him leaning against
My forearm like a mountain against a swirl of affectionate air. That's all.

A Poem for Literature Teacher Beth Morgan of Lassiter High in Georgia

Maybe you will think this is a tiny thing
But *I* do not think it's a little thing when
A student asks me if I could possibly jot
A poem for his absolute favorite teacher
Because he wants to give her an odd gift
Of a poem by a writer she enjoys and he,
The student, says he knows this is crazy,
But he *really* admires this teacher, so he,
The writer, touched by the student's guts
And how fine the teacher must be to jazz
A student like that, says sure, and he sits
Down one morning to scribble the poem,
And here it is, but this poem, you notice,
Is a poem about the student being moved
By a teacher, and the teacher being zesty
And honest and real and so passionate as
To stories that he, the student, will never
Forget the teacher. *That* is the best poem.

Poem for Dave McIrvin

I once knew a doctor who had the subtle custom of crouching
Down to eye level to talk to anyone of any age or stage. He'd
Appear suddenly, a slight intense grinning swift man, and as I
Sat down in a chair he would crouch down and look me in the
Eye. My wife was sitting next to me and he would look her in
The eyes also. This is what I remember hauntingly powerfully
This afternoon. He would often be there for quite a long while.
He was never hurried, although he always was in a wild hurry.
Trust me, he would say, and we trusted him with all our hearts
In large part because he crouched down to talk to us where we
Were. We were terrified, and he knew this, and so he made an
Effort, a tremendous effort, an effort that never failed, to come
Down to where we were huddled together in those cold chairs.
Humility is the final frontier—humility is where wisdom lives,
Isn't that so? And every genuine sign of it is unforgettable. As
You see. To crouch, to bow, to listen, to attend; it seems to me
These are prayers, and the most eloquent prayers are wordless.

How Can You Write a Poem if You Are an Essayist?

Is the blunt question this morning from a serious high school student,
And my answer is something like: sidelongingly, hesitatingly, swiftly
And then slowly. I start with an image or a line and then things sprint
Away & a story tells itself and I try to stay attentive but not in control.
Does this make any kind of sense to you? I pile up lines and they jazz
Each other and I have to keep a semblance of narrative order. A poem
Can run completely away sometimes, and I end up with either nothing
On the page or a sudden essay. Often whatever I thought I was writing
About is not what I end up writing about. All this sounds bizarre, but I
Have learned to be sharp and careless and diligent and lazy all at once.
A poem is like you rolled down hills when you were a kid—wildly but
Not completely out of control. You have an idea but you don't instruct
Or command or demand. You listen to the lines, is the closest I can get.
You are gaping at me with the exact look that I saw once on a new calf.
I cannot articulate this in a sensible and reasonable way. Poems let you
Write them, sometimes. They startle the page. They have interior notes
That you can occasionally sculpt into chords and melodies and so forth.
A poem is something that you start and then you close your eyes so you
Can see better. Does that make sense at all? No? Then I have done well.

After

A couple of months before I was due to graduate from college
I found myself sprawled on the lawn of the campus quadrangle
With a very good friend. We lay there staring up. Just up, is all.
We had not the faintest idea what we were going to do . . . after.
After was the way we referred to it. There was now, which had
Sprawled four years, and there was after. That would be a long
Time, it seemed to us. This wasn't about nostalgia, not really at
All. We were just nonplussed. That is a great word for what we
Were. Disconcerted but not all the way discombobulated. Most
Of the people we knew were either totally lined up for graduate
School or jobs or taking over their mom's bowling alley empire
Or their about-to-be-father-in-law's car-wash-and-wax business
But we were nonplussed. I suppose we talked a little about what
We might do, but I don't remember that. What I remember is an
Odd pleasure in just being sprawled in the grass. In a minute we
Will get up and soon it will be after but not just yet. Yes, we are
Muddled and worried and confused and trepidacious about what
Exactly we will do, and we do not want to let our families down,
And we want to do work that matters and is fun and maybe even
A little remunerative, but just now, for a moment, there are trees,
And this dense lovely grass, and a good friend, and a crow going
Home from work. Why is it that crows hardly ever seem hurried?
Once in a while you will see crows arrowing and intent—usually
Because they are diving on a huddled annoyed hawk—but rarely,
It seems to me. Mostly they amble along, fitting into the moment,
Isn't that so? Somehow they have the time not to fuss about time.

Seanchaí

I have delivered too many eulogies lately.
One every other month. I am moved to be
Asked, and I say yes, of course, of course,
And I take notes on stories, and I write all
The notes into a text, and then say it again
And again and again until I have it shaped
As a story in my mind. And then the black
Suit and the murmuring crowd and the shy
Grandchildren in the front row. Never stay
Behind the lectern, behind the microphone.
Deconstruct and dismantle the somber of it.
First make people laugh. Make them recall
The deceased was a goofy grinning nutball,
As are we all, as are we all. Then tell a tale.
We are all endless stories. Choose any few.
You want people to laugh, and then shuffle
Away thinking of their late friend as a verb.
Don't be religious. Someone else will cover
That base. *Shout* the thing that must be said.
What were you about? Why did people love
You? What can they keep of who you were?
What can they slip in their suit-coat pockets
And find again and again and remember you
By? Why did we love you? Say that as clear
As you possibly can. Then sit down speedily,
Ideally in the shadows. You are not the show.
You are the one chosen to say what everyone
Is thinking. This is an ancient task and honor.

You are the tongue in every mouth. In Gaelic,
The seanchaí, the storyteller, the storycatcher,
The rememberer, the singer of what is crucial.
Afterwards accept no pay; but savor the drink.

The Tale You Did Not Know
You Needed to Know

Spent an hour this morning talking to a family
Who had just lost their husband dad granddad.
I wanted to listen to them for a bit because I'm
Delivering his eulogy tomorrow and they want
To say some things. I took notes. The children
Sat munching toast. Upstairs a boy had the flu.
Juncos kept arriving at the feeder the deceased
Filled with seeds every morning until he could
Not move anymore. I took a lot of notes. Now,
Much later, I read over what I wrote and I find
One line underlined several times. <u>Anytime he
Saw someone cleaning a bathroom, if we were
Out at a restaurant or at a hotel or wherever, he
Would go shake their hands and say thank you.
I bet he did that a thousand times</u>, said his wife.
I find that if you listen, people will tell you just
The tale you did not know you needed to know.